INFUSED
BOOZE

◇◇◇

Kathy Kordalis

INFUSED
BOOZE

◇◇◇

Kathy Kordalis

Over 60 batched spirits and
liqueurs to make at home

Photography by Jacqui Melville

hardie grant books

CONTENTS

06
INTRODUCTION

08
COVER YOUR BASES

10
FLAVOURINGS

12
SERVING AND STORAGE

14
CHAPTER 1
CITRUS, SOFT FRUIT
AND RED FRUIT

44
CHAPTER 2
BLOSSOMY AND BOTANIC

58
CHAPTER 3
HERBACIOUS, VERDANT,
RESIN AND PINE

74
CHAPTER 4
STICKY, NUTTY
AND EARTHY

104
CHAPTER 5
HOT AND SPICY

124
CHAPTER 6
SYRUPS, SHRUBS AND
FLAVOURED FIZZ

138
ABOUT THE AUTHOR

139
AKNOWLEDGEMENTS

INTRODUCTION

Supermarket shelves are filled with flavoured booze, from vodka and gin, to various liqueurs. However, a lot of mass-produced flavoured alcohol products are full of artificial ingredients. By infusing your own alcohol at home, you can control the quality of the ingredients and minimise the additives. When done well, spirits infused with perfectly ripe, seasonal produce make a great addition to your liquor cabinet and can add lovely complexity when used in cocktails.

Infusing your booze is so simple, but very impressive! It involves minimum effort for maximum flavour! And you don't have to be a science whiz; all it requires is creativity and a few items of equipment. To start flavouring your alcohol, you will need a minimum of two components: a bottle of alcohol and something to infuse it with.

This book will guide you through the basics of making infused booze, and give you cocktail ideas for how to drink it! Infusions are both fun and limitless, but the basic concept of any infusion is a single or a combination of flavours mixed with a liquor.

Vodka and gin are the most common 'base' spirits, but other light liquors such as white rum, dark rum and tequila can also be used. Infusing darker spirits is a little trickier, but well worth it if you choose the right flavour to complement the booze.

There is a big difference between an infused spirit and a liqueur. In simple terms, an infusion or maceration with alcohol and added sugar is a liqueur. Sloe gin, for example, is a liqueur. An infused spirit involves the addition of fruit, flowers, herbs or other aromatics to a spirit. This book is inspired by the gin foundries' flavour notes such as Floral and Grassy, and Herbal and Piney, but experimentation is encouraged. When researching this book I found their approach to flavour quite inspiring. I have also added my own interpretation. Make the infusions your own, celebrate them, and share them with friends.

COVER YOUR BASES

When selecting the 'base' spirit for your infusion, consider what you want to flavour it with. White spirits, such as vodka, gin or white rum work with just about any flavour. There is no need to spend a fortune on the highest-quality base, just choose something with a neutral flavour that you would be happy to drink.

Brown spirits, such as dark rum and brandy, can also be infused, but they are more complex in flavour so you need to be careful when selecting your aromatics. Bolder flavourings, such as spices and nuts, go particularly well with these bases. Source a spirit that is clean-tasting and uncomplicated, and don't bankrupt yourself buying an expensive whiskey.

When it comes to choosing flowers, fruit or herbs for your infusion, there is a huge spectrum of possibility. But the best way to begin is to look at what is in season. Seasonal herbs tend to marry well with seasonal fruits, so have a look around your garden to see what is growing. Whether you're making it for yourself, or to give as a gift, personalising your infused booze is a real treat!

FLAVOURINGS

This is where you can really have some fun! Whether you use seasonal produce, or experiment with different ingredients, this book has suggestions for a range of tasty combinations, and I encourage you to have fun!

Infusing booze with your choice of flavours is a great way to make something bespoke. A cornucopia of ingredients can be used, including herbs and other botanicals; fruits, both dried and fresh; nuts; seeds; vegetables and spices.

When choosing your ingredients, try to select complementary flavour notes. Herbs such as rosemary, thyme, dill, basil and mint, and more unique botanicals such as lemon verbena, give a fresh, grassy taste.

Fresh citrus fruits, such as lime, orange and grapefruit, give infusions a hit of acidity, whereas ripe red fruit, such as strawberries, pomegranate and rhubarb, add a hint of sweetness. In the height of summer, stone fruit is ideal for giving an infusion a full, juicy flavour.

Vegetables, such as beetroot and cucumber, add a cool, clean dimension. No matter what you use, opt for approximately 200–400 g (7–14 oz) of fruit per litre (34 fl oz) of spirit to get the balance right.

For creamy, nutty and fragrant notes, try using spices, such as cardamom, ginger, nutmeg, vanilla and cloves, or more unusual ingredients, such as tonka beans. All types of chilli can add spice and heat, too. Just remember, the more you use, the stronger the flavour will be – one or two chillies are usually sufficient.

Syrups can also be used to infuse booze. Their mild flavour and sweetness is perfect for balancing an infusion, especially when using acidic fruits.

Shrubs, also known as drinking vinegars, are one of the most refreshing things you can drink and, mixed with your infused booze, they can really bring a cocktail to life. Shrubs are a delicately balanced combination of vinegar, fruit and sugar. Added to a glass with something bubbly, such as sparkling water, they make a perfect drink for the summer. Mixing them with alcohol is even better.

Infusing fizzy water is a non-alcoholic way to add some flavour to your beverage. This 'flavoured fizz' is ready in a fraction of the time it takes to make an infused booze – generally a few hours or overnight – so you can enjoy it right away.

SERVING AND STORAGE

Just about all the recipes in this book require sterilised jars. To prepare them, preheat the oven to 140°C (280°F/Gas mark 1). Wash the jars and lids in hot, soapy water, then rinse well and place the jars, mouths facing up, on a baking tray. Transfer to the oven and leave to dry out completely. Leave the lids to air-dry on a clean tea towel (dish towel).

When you're ready to start infusing, wash the ingredients well and cut them, if needed, to fit inside the jar. Combine the ingredients in the base of your jar and pour over the liquor. You may want to divide your liquor between smaller jars and experiment with a few different infusions at the same time.

Seal the jar tightly and shake a few times to mix the ingredients. Label the jars with masking tape and add notes about the ingredients, dates, and anything else you want to remember for next time.

With all infused boozes, timing is important. Here is a rough guide:

Stronger flavours, such as chilli and vanilla, should be left for approximately 24 hours. The longer you leave the infusion, the stronger (and spicier) it will be.

Spices and vegetables will need 5–7 days.

To impart their flavour, berries and other strong fruit will need 3–4 weeks.

Milder flavours, such as apple, lemongrass, melon and florals may take up to 1 month to infuse. However, I believe that taste is very personal so I highly recommend you check the booze every 2 days and strain it when it has reached a flavour you are happy with.

Once infused, strain the spirit through a fine-mesh sieve to remove the larger solids. Then strain again through a fine-mesh sieve lined with a muslin (cheesecloth) or a clean kitchen cloth to clarify the mixture. You can also use a coffee filter for this.

Using a funnel, pour your infused alcohol into one large or several smaller sterilised storage jars or bottles. You now have an infused booze that you can store in your cupboard to enjoy on its own or in cocktails.

At the end of every recipe in this book you'll find 'Cocktail Tips'. These are suggestions for how you can serve your infusions. Whether you are building mixed drinks and shaking with ice in a shaker, or simply serving over ice (on the rocks), you will have plenty of options and ideas.

A standard single measure of alcohol in the UK is 25 ml (¾ fl oz). In other parts of the world, it is 30 ml (1 fl oz). The cocktail recipes in this book use either one UK measure or one full quantity of the infused booze. As always, taste your cocktails as you go and tweak to suit your preference.

CHAPTER 1

CITRUS, SOFT FRUIT AND RED FRUIT

MARMA-ADE

Makes
700 ml (23½ fl oz)

Takes
10 minutes,
*   plus 4 days to infuse*

Ingredients
1 orange, sliced into rounds
2 clementines, sliced into rounds
600 ml (20½ fl oz)
*   unflavoured vodka*
100 ml (3½ fl oz) red vermouth
1 teaspoon orange-blossom
*   water*

When I think of citrus I think of oranges and clementines, which give this drink a classic zing and provide so much goodness! This infusion is layered with orange, clementines, and red vermouth with its aromatic flavouring of botanicals and delicate finish of orange blossom.

Put the sliced orange and clementines in a sterilised 1 litre (34 fl oz) glass jar or bottle and pour over the vodka and vermouth. Seal the jar tightly and store in a cool, dark place for 3 days, until the colour has deepened. Gently shake the jar occasionally to help infuse the flavours.

After 3 days, or once you are happy with the flavour, add the orange-blossom water and store for 1 more day to allow the vodka to absorb the flavour.

Strain the mixture through a fine-mesh sieve into a large jug, and discard the fruit. Strain again through a fine-mesh sieve lined with a muslin (cheesecloth) or a coffee filter. Transfer to one large or several smaller sterilised glass bottles and seal tightly.

COCKTAIL TIP

For a lovely Orange Fizz, pour a single measure (25 ml/¾ fl oz) Marma-ade into a glass or chilled cocktail glass and top with Champagne or prosecco. Garnish with a clementine wedge.

LIME AND LEMONGRASS RUM

Makes
700 ml (23½ fl oz)

Takes
10 minutes,
*   plus 3 days to infuse*

Ingredients
3 lemongrass stalks, bruised
3 limes, sliced into rounds
700 ml (23½ fl oz) white rum

Lemongrass is a tropical island plant in the grass family, which gets its name from its very light citrusy flavour. When married with the gentle but sour bitterness of limes and infused in rum, the combined flavours immediately evoke the spirit of sun-drenched Asian-Caribbean parties.

Put the lemongrass stalks and sliced lime in a sterilised 1 litre (34 fl oz) glass jar or bottle and pour over the rum. Seal the jar tightly and store in a cool, dark place for 3 days, gently shaking the jar occasionally to help infuse the flavours.

After 3 days, strain the infused rum through a fine-mesh sieve into a large jug, and discard the fruit. Strain again through a fine-mesh sieve lined with a muslin (cheesecloth) or a coffee filter. Transfer to one large or several smaller sterilised glass bottles and seal tightly.

COCKTAIL TIP

To make a Lime and Lemongrass Rum Jug, place 100 ml (3½ fl oz) infused rum in a large jug. Add ice cubes, lime wedges or slices and 1–2 tablespoons of runny honey, then top up with soda water. To serve, rub lime juice around the rims of chilled cocktail glasses and dip in bee pollen. Allow the bee pollen to dry before filling the glasses.

PINK GRAPEFRUIT AND HIBISCUS TEA GIN

Makes
700 ml (23½ fl oz)

Takes
20 minutes,
*   plus 3 days to infuse*

Ingredients
2–3 hibiscus tea bags
700 ml (23½ fl oz) gin
1 medium pink grapefruit,
*   cut into wedges*

Pink grapefruits fall somewhere between white and red grapefruits with their mild tangy sweetness. The addition of hibiscus tea to this infusion not only creates the most beautiful, elegant colour but a sumptuous flavour of cranberry-like, tanin undertones.

Place the hibiscus tea bags in a small saucepan with 100 ml (3½ fl oz) of the gin and heat gently for 3–5 minutes to infuse. Remove from the heat and leave to cool.

Once cooled, discard the tea bags and transfer the infused gin to a sterilised 1 litre (34 fl oz) glass jar or bottle and add the remaining gin and pink grapefruit wedges. Seal the jar tightly and store in a cool, dark place for 3 days, until the gin turns a deep pink colour. Gently shake the jar occasionally to help infuse the flavours.

After 3 days, strain the gin through a fine-mesh sieve into a large jug, and discard the fruit. Strain again through a fine-mesh sieve lined with a muslin (cheesecloth) or a coffee filter. Transfer to one large or several smaller sterilised glass bottles and seal tightly.

COCKTAIL TIPS

To make a Pink Hibiscus, half-fill a cocktail shaker with ice and pour in 2 measures (50 ml/1¾ fl oz) infused gin and 1 tablespoon dry vermouth. Shake well, then strain into a chilled martini glass. Place a preserved hibiscus flower and 1 teaspoon hibiscus syrup (available from specialist food stores) on top, to. Or, garnish with a slice of pink grapefruit and an edible flower.

A single measure of this gin is also delicious topped up with Prosecco.

LEMON VERBENA TEQUILA

Makes
700 ml (23½ fl oz)

Takes
10 minutes,
*   plus 3 days to infuse*

Ingredients
4 lemon verbena sprigs
1 tablespoon Simple
*   Syrup (p. 127)*
700 ml (23½ fl oz) tequila

The lemon verbena herb packs a real punch! Its strong lemon-lime flavour also has a fruity aroma, which infuses perfectly with tequila. Use it as the base of a cocktail or slam it neat from a shot glass!

Put the lemon verbena and simple syrup in a sterilised 1 litre (34 fl oz) glass jar or bottle and pour over the tequila. Seal the jar tightly and store in a cool, dark place for 3 days, gently shaking the jar occasionally to help infuse the flavours.

Strain the tequila through a fine-mesh sieve into a large jug, and discard the herbs. Strain again through a fine-mesh sieve lined with a muslin (cheesecloth) or a coffee filter. Transfer to one large or several smaller sterilised glass bottles and seal tightly.

COCKTAIL TIPS

To make a Verbena Cocktail, combine a single measure (25 ml/¾ fl oz) infused tequila with fresh verbena leaves, Ginger Syrup (p. 127) and a touch of yuzu juice, then build over ice.

To make a Mexican Revolver, add a single measure of infused tequila to a chilled Champagne flute, top with prosecco and garnish with a jalapeño chilli.

BRANDYTOPF

Makes
700 ml (23½ fl oz)

Takes
10 minutes,
*   plus 3 days to infuse*

Ingredients
200 g (7 oz) mixed citrus fruits
*   (e.g. oranges, lemons, limes,*
clementines and grapefruit), sliced
3 fresh bay leaves
1 cinnamon stick
½ nutmeg, freshly ground
6 peppercorns
700 ml (23½ fl oz) brandy

Brandytopf is based on a traditional Germanic way of preserving fruit in alcohol, called Rumtopf. Using rum as its base, the alcohol-infused fruit was eaten as a Christmas dessert. Of course, the infused rum was drunk too. Here, I have used brandy and citrus instead.

Combine the sliced citrus, bay leaves and spices in a sterilised 1 litre (34 fl oz) glass jar or bottle and pour over the brandy. Seal the jar tightly and store in a cool, dark place for 3 days, gently shaking the jar occasionally to help infuse the flavours. It's always great to taste the infusion every few days until you are happy with the flavour – it's ready when you like it!

After 3 days, strain the brandy through a fine-mesh sieve into a large jug, and discard the fruit and spices. Strain again through a fine-mesh sieve lined with a muslin (cheesecloth) or a coffee filter. Transfer to one large or several smaller sterilised glass bottles and seal tightly.

COCKTAIL TIPS

Mix a single measure (25 ml/¾ fl oz) infused brandy with black tea and serve warm with sliced citrus and a cinnamon stick.

For a Brandy Julep, mix a single measure of infused brandy with 25 ml (¾ fl oz) dark rum and 1 tablespoon Simple Syrup (p. 127), or to taste. Add 25 ml (¾ fl oz) water and some ice to a glass and pour in the liquor. Top with a mint sprig.

PEACH AND APRICOT ARMAGNAC

Makes
700 ml (23½ fl oz)

Takes
10 minutes,
   plus 3 days to infuse

Ingredients
2 peaches, stones removed
   and cut into wedges
3 apricots, stones removed
   and cut into wedges
700 ml (23½ fl oz) Armagnac

Armagnac is distilled from grapes from the region of Gascony in France. It has the subtle flavour of quince and apricot, which means it blends well with the fleshy fruit of peaches and apricots, combined in this infusion.

Put the peaches and apricots in a sterilised 1 litre (34 fl oz) glass jar or bottle and pour over the Armagnac. Seal the jar tightly and store in a cool, dark place for 3 days, gently shaking the jar occasionally to help infuse the flavours.

After 3 days, strain the Armagnac through a fine-mesh sieve into a large jug, and discard the fruit. Strain again through a fine-mesh sieve lined with a muslin (cheesecloth) or a coffee filter. Transfer to one large or several smaller sterilised glass bottles and seal tightly.

COCKTAIL TIPS

Make a Champeach by adding a single measure (25 ml/¾ fl oz) infused Armagnac to a chilled champagne flute and top with Champagne.

To make a Marvin, combine a single measure of infused Armagnac with a dash of Angostura bitters and build over ice. Garnish with a slice of orange.

MANGO AND TARRAGON VODKA

Makes
700 ml (23½ fl oz)

Takes
10 minutes,
*   plus 3 days to infuse*

Ingredients
1 mango, cleaned and sliced
3 tarragon sprigs
700 ml (23½ fl oz)
*   unflavoured vodka*

As mangoes ripen, their flavour mellows into a unique, creamy sweetness. Tarragon has a bittersweet flavour that is similar to aniseed, making this a subtle and arresting combination of flavours.

Put the sliced mango and tarragon in a sterilised 1 litre (34 fl oz) glass jar or bottle and pour over the vodka. Seal the jar tightly and store in a cool, dark place for 3 days, gently shaking the jar occasionally to help infuse the flavours.

After 3 days, strain the vodka through a fine-mesh sieve into a large jug, and discard the fruit. Strain again through a fine-mesh sieve lined with a muslin (cheesecloth) or a coffee filter. Transfer to one large or several smaller sterilised glass bottles and seal tightly.

COCKTAIL TIPS

Make a Mango-tini by mixing a single measure (25 ml/¾ fl oz) infused vodka with 50 ml (1¾ fl oz) lemon juice and 50 ml (1¾ fl oz) mango purée, then serve with fresh tarragon sprigs, to garnish.

To make Peach and Mango Sangria, add a single measure (50 ml/1¾ fl oz) Mango and Tarragon Vodka to a large jug and top with viognier. Garnish with sliced peaches and chopped mango.

GREEN MELON VODKA

Makes
700 ml (23½ fl oz)

Takes
10 minutes,
*   plus 3 days to infuse*

Ingredients
1 honeydew melon,
*   peeled and cut into wedges*
2 strips lime zest
100 ml (3½ fl oz) Midori
700 ml (23½ fl oz)
*   unflavoured vodka*

With its sweet and juicy flesh, the honeydew melon is perfect for a vodka infusion. Midori (the Japanese word for green) is a melon-flavoured liqueur, which works perfectly with the fresh melon to intensify its taste and create both a fun tipple and perfect base for cocktails.

Put the melon, lime zest and Midori in a sterilised 1 litre (34 fl oz) glass jar or bottle and pour over the vodka. Seal the jar tightly and store in a cool, dark place for 3 days, until the vodka turns a pretty green colour. Gently shake the jar occasionally to help infuse the flavours.

After 3 days, strain the vodka through a fine-mesh sieve into a large jug, and discard the fruit and zest. Strain again through a fine-mesh sieve lined with a muslin (cheesecloth) or a coffee filter. Transfer to one large or several smaller sterilised glass bottles and seal tightly.

COCKTAIL TIPS

For a Melon Cucumber-tini, add 2 measures (50 ml/1¾ fl oz) infused vodka and ½ chopped cucumber to a cocktail shaker. Using the back of a spoon, bruise the cucumber to release its juice and leave to sit for 30 minutes. Top with 1 teaspoon Simple Syrup (p. 127), or to taste, then top up with ice. Shake well, pour 50 ml (1¾ fl oz) water into the shaker, then strain into a chilled cocktail glass.

To make a Melon Patch, mix a single measure of infused vodka with 25 ml (¾ fl oz) triple sec. Serve in a chilled cocktail glass with melon balls, mini kiwi fruit and ice, and top up with soda water.

CUCUMBER, LIME AND CORIANDER-SEED GIN

Makes
700 ml (23½ fl oz)

Takes
10 minutes,
  plus 3 days to infuse

Ingredients
2 cucumbers, thinly sliced
  lengthways
1 lime, thinly sliced
1 tablespoon coriander
  (cilantro) seeds
1–3 tablespoons
Simple Syrup (p. 127)
700 ml (23½ fl oz) gin

Nothing epitomises freshness like cucumber and lime, while the addition of coriander (cilantro) seeds gives this infusion an intriguing, slightly spicy flavour that is reminscent of both citrus peel and sage.

Put the cucumber, lime, coriander seeds and Simple Syrup in a sterilised 1 litre (34 fl oz) glass jar or bottle and pour over the gin. Seal the jar tightly and store in a cool, dark place for 3 days, gently shaking the jar occasionally to help infuse the flavours.

After 3 days, strain the gin through a fine-mesh sieve into a large jug, and discard the fruit and seeds. Strain again through a fine-mesh sieve lined with a muslin (cheesecloth) or a coffee filter. Transfer to one large or several smaller sterilised glass bottles and seal tightly.

COCKTAIL TIP

Muddle some cucumber and lime in a highball glass with ice and a single measure (25 ml/¾ fl oz) infused gin, then top with ginger beer for a refreshing Cucumber and Ginger Sparkle.

GREEN APPLE, GINGER AND YUZU VODKA

Makes
700 ml (23½ fl oz)

Takes
10 minutes,
  plus 4-5 days to infuse

Ingredients
2 green apples, thinly sliced
2½ cm (1 in) piece ginger,
  peeled and thinly sliced
700 ml (23½ fl oz)
  unflavoured vodka
1 tablespoon yuzu juice

Green apples are naturally more acidic than other varieties, with a crisp, sharp taste. Combined with the aromatic and warm qualities of ginger and the floral fragrance of yuzu, the tang of the apple gives a spark to this infusion of flavours.

Put the sliced apple and ginger in a sterilised 1 litre (34 fl oz) glass jar or bottle and pour over the vodka. Seal the jar tightly and store in a cool, dark place for 3 days, gently shaking the jar occasionally to help infuse the flavours.

After 3 days, add the yuzu juice and leave to continue infusing. After 1-2 days, strain the vodka through a fine-mesh sieve into a large jug, and discard the apple and ginger. Strain again through a fine-mesh sieve lined with a muslin (cheesecloth) or a coffee filter. Transfer to one large or several smaller sterilised glass bottles and seal tightly.

COCKTAIL TIPS

To make The Apple Blossom, serve a single measure (25 ml/¾ fl oz) infused vodka with 1–2 teaspoons Simple Syrup (p. 127), garnished with fresh apple slices and apple blossom flowers.

For an Apple Sparkle, combine 350 ml (12 fl oz) Green Apple, Ginger and Yuzu Vodka with iced sparkling water, fresh apple slices and mint sprigs in a jug.

STRAWBERRY AND RHUBARB RUM

Makes
400 ml (13½ fl oz)

Takes
1 hour,
*   plus 3 days to infuse*

Ingredients
100 g (3½ oz/⅔ cup)
*   strawberries, hulled*
*   and sliced*
1 rhubarb stalk, halved
1 vanilla pod, split lengthways
*   and seeds scraped*
80 ml (2½ fl oz) Strawberry and
*   Rhubarb Shrub (see below)*
320 ml (11 fl oz) white rum

Strawberry and Rhubarb Shrub
250 g (9 oz/1⅔ cups)
*   strawberries, hulled*
*   and chopped*
250 g (9 oz/2 cups)
*   rhubarb, thinly sliced*
100 g (3½ oz/½ cup)
*   light brown sugar*
pinch of salt
2 tablespoons balsamic vinegar
200 ml (7 fl oz)
*   white wine vinegar*

A zingy, fruity and refreshing infusion, adding the shrub gives another element to this drink. Shrubs, a concoction of vinegar, fruit and sugar, are very versatile and help to retain the true flavour of fruits like strawberry and rhubarb, bringing a lovely effervescence to any cocktail.

To make the shrub, combine the strawberries, rhubarb, sugar, salt and balsamic vinegar in a saucepan. Place over medium heat and cook, stirring occasionally, until the mixture comes to a simmer and the fruit begins to break down. Reduce the heat to low, add the white wine vinegar, then cover and cook for about 15 minutes, or until the fruit has softened and released all of its juices.

Remove from the heat and leave to cool to room temperature. Strain the mixture through a fine-mesh sieve and discard the fruit pulp. Refrigerate the shrub in an airtight container for up to 1 week or use straight away.

Put the strawberries, rhubarb stalk, vanilla pod and seeds, and shrub in a sterilised 1 litre (34 fl oz) glass jar or bottle and pour over the rum. Seal the jar tightly and store in the refrigerator for 3 days, gently shaking the jar occasionally to help infuse the flavours.

After 3 days, strain the rum through a fine-mesh sieve, and discard the rhubarb stalk and strawberries. Strain again through a fine-mesh sieve lined with a muslin (cheesecloth) or a coffee filter. Use straight away.

COCKTAIL TIPS

For a Summertime Garden Shrub, fill a highball glass with ice cubes, add a single measure (25 ml/¾ fl oz) infused rum and a single measure (25 ml/¾ fl oz) Strawberry and Rhubarb Shrub (see left). Add Simple Syrup (p. 127) to taste, then top with soda water and garnish with a few whole strawberries and a piece of rhubarb peel.

To make a Sweet and Sour Strawberry Rhubarb Daiquiri, combine 100 ml (3½ fl oz) strawberry purée with the juice of ½ lime, 1–2 teaspoons Simple Syrup (p. 127), or to taste, and a single measure of infused rum in a cocktail shaker. Shake briefly, then strain into a cocktail glass.

CHERRY GIN

Makes

700 ml (23½ fl oz)

Takes

45 minutes,
    plus 3 days to infuse

Ingredients

200 g (7 oz/1⅓ cups) fresh dark
    cherries, pitted
100 ml (3½ fl oz) Cherry
    Syrup (see below)
600 ml (20½ fl oz) gin

Cherry Syrup

200 g (7 oz /1⅓ cups) fresh
    cherries, pitted
200 g (7 oz/1⅓ cups) caster
    (superfine) sugar
juice of ½ lemon

There is something very luxurious about the deep colour and taste of cherries in alcohol. This infusion of cherry syrup and fresh cherries celebrates this depth of flavour, too.

To make the Cherry Syrup, combine the cherries, sugar and lemon juice with 100 ml (3½ fl oz) water in a saucepan over medium heat. Bring to a simmer and cook for 30 minutes. Strain the syrup through a fine-mesh sieve and discard the fruit. Store the syrup in an airtight container in the refrigerator for up to 7 days.

Put the dark cherries in a sterilised 1 litre (34 fl oz) glass jar or bottle and pour over the Cherry Syrup and gin. Seal the jar tightly and store in a cool, dark place for 3 days, gently shaking the jar occasionally to help infuse the flavours.

After 3 days, strain the gin through a fine-mesh sieve into a large jug, and discard the fruit. Strain again through a fine-mesh sieve lined with a muslin (cheesecloth) or a coffee filter. Transfer to one large or several smaller sterilised glass bottles and seal tightly.

COCKTAIL TIPS

For a Cherry Gin Sling, combine 350 ml (12 fl oz) Cherry Gin, 25 ml (¾ fl oz) Cointreau, 2–3 dashes Angostura bitters and the juice of ½ lime in a jug. Top up with soda water and mix well.

Serve 1 quantity of infused gin and 1 quantity of Cherry Syrup with a cherry garnish and allow guests to make their own drinks.

RASPBERRY, REDCURRANT AND VANILLA VODKA

Makes
700 ml (23½ fl oz)

Takes
10 minutes,
*   plus 3 days to infuse*

Ingredients
300 g (10½ oz/1½ cups)
*   raspberries*
100 g (3½ oz/⅔ cup) redcurrants
2 vanilla pods, split lengthways
*   and seeds scraped*
1 tablespoon Simple Syrup (p. 127)
700 ml (23½ fl oz)
*   unflavoured vodka*

The sweet piquancy of fresh redcurrants and raspberries is enhanced by the softness of the vanilla in this delicious vodka infusion. Not only brilliant for cocktails, you can use it to flavour desserts like a classic boozy trifle as well.

Put the raspberries, redcurrants, vanilla pods and seeds and Simple Syrup in a sterilised 1 litre (34 fl oz) glass jar or bottle and pour over the vodka. Seal the jar tightly and store in a cool, dark place for 3 days, until the vodka turns a pretty pink colour. Gently shake the jar occasionally to help infuse the flavours.

After 3 days, strain the vodka through a fine-mesh sieve into a large jug, and discard the fruit and vanilla pods. Strain again through a fine-mesh sieve lined with a muslin (cheesecloth) or a coffee filter. Transfer to one large or several smaller sterilised glass bottles and seal tightly.

COCKTAIL TIPS

Serve a single measure (25 ml/¾ fl oz) infused vodka cold in a chilled cocktail glass, garnished with a vanilla pod.

To make a Spiked Raspberry Soda, add 2 measures (50 ml/ 1¾ fl oz) infused vodka to a glass with ice. Add 50 g (1¾ oz) fresh raspberries and 2 lime wedges and top up with iced soda water.

CRANBERRY-SPICED WHISKEY

Makes
660 ml (22½ fl oz)

Takes
10 minutes,
plus 3 days to infuse

Ingredients
200 g (7 oz/2 cups) fresh
or frozen cranberries
1 cinnamon stick
2 star anise
2 cardamom pods, bruised
1 vanilla pods, split lengthways
and seeds scraped
60 ml (2 fl oz) agave syrup,
to taste
600 ml (20½ fl oz) whiskey

Perfect for the festive season of Christmas time, this infusion is spicy, tart and heady and can be used for a hot toddy as well as served refreshingly cold.

Put the cranberries, cinnamon, star anise, cardamom, vanilla pods and seeds and agave in a sterilised 1 litre (34 fl oz) glass jar or bottle and pour over the whiskey. Seal the jar tightly and store in a cool, dark place for 3 days, gently shaking the jar occasionally to help infuse the flavours.

After 3 days, strain the whiskey through a fine-mesh sieve into a large jug, and discard the fruit and spices. Strain again through a fine-mesh sieve lined with a muslin (cheesecloth) or a coffee filter. Transfer to one large or several smaller sterilised glass bottles and seal tightly.

COCKTAIL TIPS

Serve a single measure (25 ml/¾ fl oz) infused whiskey in a tumbler over ice, garnished with fresh cranberries and a cinnamon stick for The Cranberry Spice.

For Christmas, add a single measure of infused whiskey to a mug of warm mulled wine.

CHAPTER 2

◇◇◇

BLOSSOMY
AND BOTANIC

ROSE, STRAWBERRY AND RED GRAPEFRUIT WINE

Makes
700 ml (23½ fl oz)

Takes
10 minutes,
*   plus 1 day to infuse*

Ingredients
100 g (3½ oz/⅔ cup) strawberries,
*   hulled and sliced*
1 medium red grapefruit,
*   sliced into rounds*
1 rosehip sprig, optional (if
*   in season)*
1 teaspoon rosewater
700 ml (23½ fl oz) rosé
*   blush wine*

This is my favourite summer drink by far. Whether it's an Aperol Spritz or just served as a glass of infused rosé wine, it's super special! If rosehip is in season, add a sprig to elevate the taste further, while the addition of rose water gives an elegant floral aroma to the end result, making this a drink with many distinct and delicious layers.

Put the strawberries, sliced grapefruit and rosewater in a sterilised 1 litre (34 fl oz) glass jar or bottle and pour over the rosé. Seal the jar tightly and store in the refrigerator overnight, gently shaking the jar occasionally to help infuse the flavours.

When you're ready to serve, strain the rosé through a fine-mesh sieve lined with a muslin (cheesecloth) into a large jug, and discard the fruit.

COCKTAIL TIPS

Add sparkling water to 1 quantity Rose, Strawberry and Red Grapefruit Wine, and garnish with rose petals.

For a Rose Aperol Spritz, mix 200 ml (7 fl oz) infused rosé with 25 ml (¾ fl oz) Aperol and garnish with a slice of grapefruit.

JASMINE TEA AND ELDERFLOWER GIN

Makes
700 ml (23½ fl oz)

Takes
*45 minutes,
    plus 3 days to infuse*

Ingredients
*2–3 jasmine tea bags
600 ml (20½ fl oz) gin
100 ml (3½ fl oz)
    elderflower cordial*

Jasmine and elderflower combined creates a delightfully perfumed bouquet, fragrant yet delicate and subtle. As a flavoured gin, this is wonderful on its own over ice. To give it a twist, muddle with lots of lime and mint and add a dash of Angostura bitters, to create a powerful flavour spectrum.

Place the tea bags and 100 ml (3½ fl oz) of the gin in a saucepan. Set over low heat and gently infuse for 30 minutes. Remove from the heat and leave to cool.

Transfer the cooled gin to a sterilised 1 litre (34 fl oz) glass jar or bottle and pour over the remaining gin and cordial. Seal the jar tightly and store in a cool, dark place for 3 days, until the vodka is a deep pink colour. Gently shake the jar occasionally to help infuse the flavours.

After 3 days, strain the gin through a fine-mesh sieve into a large jug, and discard the tea bags. Strain again through a fine-mesh sieve lined with a muslin (cheesecloth) or a coffee filter. Transfer to one large or several smaller sterilised glass bottles and seal tightly.

COCKTAIL TIPS

To make The Jasmine, combine 25 ml (¾ fl oz) Campari and 25 ml (¾ fl oz) Cointreau with a single measure (25 ml/¾ fl oz) infused gin in a cocktail shaker. Add ice, shake briefly and strain into a chilled cocktail glass. Garnish with a lemon twist.

Add muddled lime and mint and a dash of Angostura bitters to a single measure of infused gin for a Jasmine Sour.

VIOLET AND BLUEBERRY VODKA

Makes
700 ml (23½ fl oz)

Takes
30 minutes,
*   plus 4 days to infuse*

Ingredients
200 g (7 oz/1¼ cups) blueberries
100 ml (3½ fl oz) Violet Syrup
*   (see below) or 200 g*
*   (7 oz/2 cups) fresh*
*   edible violets*
2 strips orange zest
1 vanilla pods, split lenthways
*   and seeds scraped*
700 ml (23½ fl oz) unflavoured
vodka

Violet Syrup
300 g (10½ oz/3 cups) fresh
*   edible violets, loosely*
*   packed*
300 g (10½ oz/1½ cups)
*   granulated sugar*
squeeze of lemon juice

Violets have been used throughout history to flavour and decorate food. They impart a mild sweetness but it is really the colour that's so impressive. For this recipe, ensure you only use ordinary blue or purple woodland violets or scented, cultivated violets. Never use the African violets popular as houseplants; they are members of an entirely different plant family, *Saintpaulia*, and are inedible.

To make the Violet Syrup, thoroughly wash the violets under cool running water, then carefully remove the green leaves and stems.

Bring 250 ml (8½ fl oz) water to the boil in a small saucepan over high heat. Add the sugar and stir until the sugar has dissolved. Remove from the heat and add the violets, then cover and leave to sit for 24 hours. Strain the violet-infused liquid through a fine-mesh sieve, gently pressing the violets with a spoon to extract any additional liquid. Do not allow it to infuse for too long as you will lose the gorgeous colour of the violets. Stir in the lemon juice, a drop at a time. This will make the infusion a clear purple colour.

Put the blueberries, Violet Syrup or fresh violets, orange zest and vanilla pods and seeds in a sterilised 1 litre (34 fl oz) glass jar or bottle and pour over the vodka. Seal the jar tightly and store in a cool, dark place for 3 days, until the vodka turns violet. Gently shake the jar occasionally to infuse the flavours.

After 3 days, strain the vodka through a fine-mesh sieve into a large jug, and discard the solids. Strain again through a fine-mesh sieve lined with a muslin (cheesecloth) or a coffee filter. Transfer to one large or several smaller sterilised glass bottles and seal tightly.

COCKTAIL TIP

To make Violet Blueberry Champagne with Sorbet, place a scoop of passion fruit sorbet in the bottom of a cocktail glass. Add a single measure (25 ml/¾ fl oz) infused vodka and top with Champagne.

KAFFIR LIME, LEMONGRASS AND GINGER RUM

Makes
700 ml (23½ fl oz)

Takes
10 minutes,
   plus 6 days to infuse

Ingredients
1 handful kaffir lime leaves
700 ml (23½ fl oz) white rum
2 lemongrass stalks, bruised
1 thumb ginger, peeled and sliced

Reminiscent of many a fun-filled holiday, this rum infusion is also a great accompaniment to a Thai curry, whether just over ice or as a long drink with soda. My absolute favourite is to shake it up with some mango purée – so delicious!

Put the kaffir lime leaves in a sterilised 1 litre (34 fl oz) glass jar or bottle and pour over the rum. Seal the jar tightly and store in a cool, dark place for 3 days, gently shaking the jar occasionally to help infuse the flavours.

After 3 days, add the lemongrass and sliced ginger to the rum. Seal and store for a further 3 days, to allow the rum to absorb the flavours.

Strain the rum through a fine-mesh sieve into a large jug, and discard the solids. Strain again through a fine-mesh sieve lined with a muslin (cheesecloth) or a coffee filter. Transfer to one large or several smaller sterilised glass bottles and seal tightly.

COCKTAIL TIP

For a Mangosit, add 2 measures (50 ml/1¾ fl oz) infused rum to a cocktail shaker with 150 ml (5 fl oz) mango purée and top up with ice. Shake briefly, strain into a chilled cocktail glass and garnish with an edible violet.

FENNEL AND CARDAMOM AQUAVIT

Makes
760 ml (26¾ fl oz)

Takes
10 minutes,
*   plus 3 days to infuse*

Ingredients
1 fennel bulb with fronds, sliced
3 cardamom pods, bruised
60 ml (2 fl oz) Simple
*   Syrup (p. 127)*
700 ml (23½ fl oz) aquavit

Scandinavian aquavit is flavoured with herbs, spices and fruits during the distilling process. The main flavours are caraway, cardamom, cumin, anise and fennel, and my preference is to infuse with fennel and cardamom, ramping up these flavours. Serve simply over ice and garnished with frozen lingonberries to make a modern Scandi drink.

Put the fennel, cardamom and simple syrup in a sterilised 1 litre (34 fl oz) glass jar or bottle and pour over the aquavit. Seal the jar tightly and store in a cool, dark place for 3 days, gently shaking the jar occasionally to help infuse the flavours.

After 3 days, strain the aquavit through a fine-mesh sieve into a large jug, and discard the fennel and cardamom. Strain again through a fine-mesh sieve lined with a muslin (cheesecloth) or a coffee filter. Transfer to one large or several smaller sterilised glass bottles and seal tightly.

COCKTAIL TIPS

For a Blood Orange Mary with Aquavit, combine 2 measures (50 ml/1¾ fl oz) infused aquavit with 250 ml (8½ fl oz) blood orange juice. Mix in a dash of Worcestershire sauce and a dash of Tabasco. Pour into a highball glass and garnish with a slice of fennel.

Make a Lingonberry Aquavit by adding a single measure (25 ml/¾ fl oz) infused aquavit to a highball glass. Top up with soda water and garnish with a sprig of fresh dill and a handful of frozen lingonberries (available at Scandinavian and health shops).

OREGANO AND LEMON-INFUSED PISCO

Makes
600 ml (20½ fl oz)

Takes
10 minutes,
*   plus 3 days to infuse*

Ingredients
3 oregano sprigs
3 lemons, washed
*   and cut into wedges*
600 ml (20½ fl oz) pisco

Pisco is an unaged, Peruvian brandy made from grapes. It's extremely light with a gently sweet aftertaste, while oregano's pungent green flavour and lemon gives this a tangy zing.

Put the oregano and lemon in a sterilised 1 litre (34 fl oz) glass jar or bottle and pour over the pisco. Seal the jar tightly and store in a cool, dark place for 3 days, gently shaking the jar occasionally to help infuse the flavours.

After 3 days, strain the pisco through a fine-mesh sieve into a large jug, and discard the lemon and oregano. Strain again through a fine-mesh sieve lined with a muslin (cheesecloth) or a coffee filter. Transfer to one large or several smaller sterilised glass bottles and seal tightly.

COCKTAIL TIPS

To make a Cobbler, mix 2 measures (50 ml/1¾ fl oz) infused pisco with 25 ml (¾ fl oz) dry vermouth, 1 teaspoon Simple Syrup (p. 127) and the juice of ¼ lemon, then build in a cocktail glass over ice. Garnish with an oregano sprig and a lemon twist.

For an Oregano Pisco Sour, half-fill a cocktail shaker with ice and add 100 ml (3½ fl oz) infused pisco with 1 teaspoon Simple Syrup (p. 127), the juice of ½ lime, 1–2 dashes Angostura bitters and 1 egg white. Shake vigorously, until a thick white foam forms, then strain into a glass (with the foam). Garnish with fresh oregano leaves.

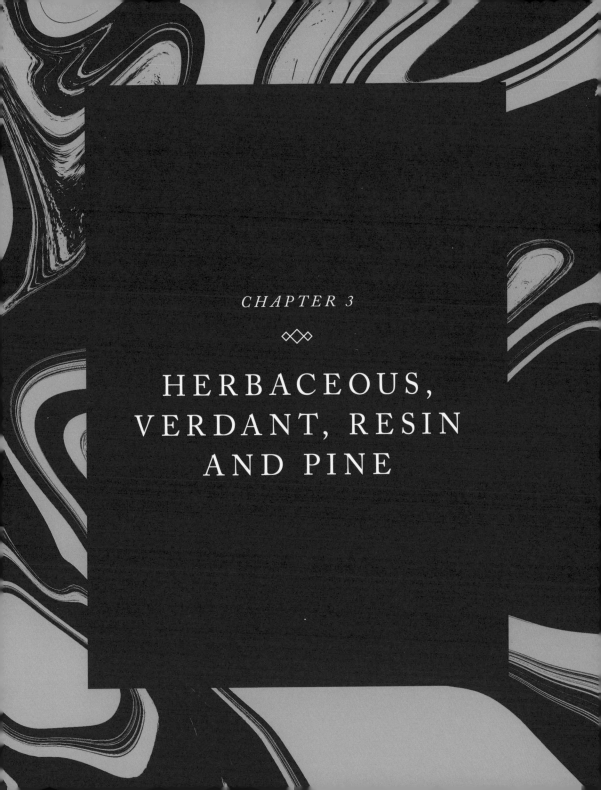

CHAPTER 3

◇◇◇

HERBACEOUS, VERDANT, RESIN AND PINE

ROASTED LEMON AND BAY VODKA

Makes
700 ml (23½ fl oz)

Takes
1 hour 30 minutes,
*   plus 3 days to infuse*

Ingredients
5 lemons, cut into quarters
1 large bunch fresh bay leaves
700 ml (23½ fl oz)
*   unflavoured vodka*
2 tablespoons light brown sugar
1 vanilla pod, split lengthways
*   and seeds scraped*

One of the most versatile of herbs, and the most quintessential of ingredients in any cook's larder, bay leaves offer a woody, herbal aroma when roasted with lemons – which deepens and mellows both flavours.

Preheat the oven to 150°C (300°F/Gas mark 2).

Place the lemons and bay leaves on a baking tray and transfer to the oven. Roast for 1 hour. After 30 minutes, sprinkle over 4 tablespoons of the vodka.

Remove from the oven and leave to cool. Transfer the cooled lemons and bay leaves to a sterilised 1 litre (34 fl oz) glass jar or bottle and pour over the remaining vodka. Add the sugar and vanilla pod and seeds. Seal the jar tightly and store in a cool, dark place for 3 days, gently shaking the jar occasionally to help infuse the flavours.

After 3 days, strain the vodka through a fine-mesh sieve into a large jug, and discard the fruit and herbs. Strain again through a fine-mesh sieve lined with a muslin (cheesecloth) or a coffee filter. Transfer to one large or several smaller sterilised glass bottles and seal tightly.

COCKTAIL TIPS

Mix 2 measures (50 ml/1¾ fl oz) infused vodka with 1 teaspoon Simple Syrup (p. 127) and the juice of ½ lemon. Build over ice in a highball glass.

For a Peace, mix 2 measures of infused vodka with 150 ml (5 fl oz) sweet Madeira and 2–3 dashes Angostura bitters in a cocktail glass. This is based on the Shalom – which means peace in Hebrew.

LEMON THYME AND HONEY-INFUSED GIN

Makes
800 ml (27 fl oz)

Takes
20 minutes,
*   plus 3 days to infuse*

Ingredients
1 bunch lemon thyme
100 ml (3½ fl oz) Honey Syrup
*   (see below)*
700 ml (23½ fl oz) gin

Honey Syrup
200 g (7 oz/ ¾ cup) honey
200 ml (7 fl oz) water

Combining it with honey is a classic way to release the subtle flavours of thyme and this gin infusion makes a very elegant tipple when topped with a chilled, crisp Riesling.

First, make the Honey Syrup. Heat the honey in a small saucepan over medium heat. Add the water and stir until thoroughly combined. Remove from the heat and leave to cool. Store the syrup in the refrigerator for up to 1 month.

Put the lemon thyme and honey syrup in a sterilised 1 litre (34 fl oz) glass jar or bottle and pour over the gin. Seal the jar tightly and store in a cool, dark place for 3 days, gently shaking the jar occasionally to help infuse the flavours.

After 3 days, strain the gin through a fine-mesh sieve into a large jug and discard the thyme. Strain again through a fine-mesh sieve lined with a muslin (cheesecloth) or a coffee filter. Transfer to one large or several smaller sterilised glass bottles and seal tightly.

COCKTAIL TIPS

Add a single measure (25 ml/¾ fl oz) infused gin to a cocktail glass and top with Riesling. Garnish with a thyme sprig and a slice of lemon.

To make a Gin and Grapefruit Gimlet, combine 2 measures (50 ml/1¾ fl oz) infused gin with 100 ml (3½ fl oz) grapefruit juice. Rub the rim of a cocktail glass with grapefruit juice and dip in finely grated grapefruit zest mixed with sugar. Fill the glass and garnish with a thyme sprig.

BASIL RUM

Makes
700 ml (23½ fl oz)

Takes
10 minutes,
*   plus 3 days to infuse*

Ingredients
1 bunch basil
1–2 tablespoons agave syrup
700 ml (23½ fl oz) white rum

Fresh basil is initially peppery but evolves into a sweet and aromatic flavour. Infused in rum, this makes a perfect base for a Strawberry and Basil Daquiri.

Put the basil and agave in a sterilised 1 litre (34 fl oz) glass jar or bottle and pour over the rum. Seal the jar tightly and store in a cool, dark place for 3 days, gently shaking the jar occasionally to help infuse the flavours.

After 3 days, strain the rum through a fine-mesh sieve into a large jug, and discard the basil. Strain again through a fine-mesh sieve lined with a muslin (cheesecloth) or a coffee filter. Transfer to one large or several smaller sterilised glass bottles and seal tightly.

COCKTAIL TIPS

Mix a single measure (25 ml/¾ fl oz) of infused rum with the juice of ½ lemon and 1 teaspoon Simple Syrup (p. 127) in a cocktail glass. Garnish with a basil leaf and a piece of dried pineapple.

To make a Strawberry and Basil Daiquiri, blitz 100 g (3½ oz/⅔ cup) strawberries to a smooth purée using a hand-held blender. Mix with a single measure of infused rum and pour into a martini glass. Garnish with a basil leaf.

MINT, POMEGRANATE AND FIG GIN

Makes

700 ml (23½ fl oz)

Takes

10 minutes,
*   plus 3 days to infuse*

Ingredients

200 g (7 oz/1 cup) pomegranate
*   seeds*
30 g (1 oz/1½ cups) mint leaves
3 figs, halved
2 teaspoons Honey Syrup (p. 62)
700 ml (23½ fl oz) gin

Pomegranates, mint, figs and honey create a luxurious synergy of flavours and also look beautiful in the jar, making this infusion a lovely gift for someone.

Put the pomegranate seeds, mint, figs and Honey Syrup in a sterilised 1 litre (34 fl oz) glass jar or bottle and pour over the gin. Seal the jar tightly and store in a cool, dark place for 3 days, gently shaking the jar occasionally to help infuse the flavours.

After 3 days, strain the gin through a fine-mesh sieve into a large jug, and discard the solids. Strain again through a fine-mesh sieve lined with a muslin (cheesecloth) or a coffee filter. Transfer to one large or several smaller sterilised glass bottles and seal tightly.

COCKTAIL TIPS

Add a single measure (25 ml/¾ fl oz) infused gin to a cocktail shaker with 20 ml (¾ fl oz) grenadine, 1 bruised cardamom pod, the juice of ½ lemon and some ice. Shake briefly, then strain into a chilled cocktail glass and garnish with pomegranate seeds and a mint sprig.

Mix a single measure of infused gin into a cup of fresh mint tea and serve with fresh figs and Turkish delight (loukoumia) on the side.

SMOKED ROSEMARY RUM

Makes
700 ml (23½ fl oz)

Takes
45 minutes,
*   plus 3 days to infuse*

Ingredients
100 ml (3½ fl oz) Smoked
*   Rosemary Citrus Syrup*
*   (see below)*
2 smoked rosemary stalks
700 ml (23½ fl oz) rum

Smoked Rosemary
Citrus Syrup
250 g (9 oz/1¼ cups) caster
*   (superfine) sugar*
zest and juice of 2 lemons
zest and juice of 2 limes
4 rosemary sprigs

Smoking the rosemary before adding it to this infusion really enhances its distinctive piney aroma. It's so easy to do, but really creates an impressive depth to the flavour.

For the Smoked Rosemary Citrus Syrup, combine the sugar, 250 ml (8½ fl oz) water, citrus zest and juice in a saucepan over medium–high heat. Stir, bringing it to just under boiling point, then remove from heat and cover with a lid.

Meanwhile, hold the rosemary over an open flame using heatproof tongs. Turn continually until it begins to smoke, being careful not to let it catch, then transfer immediately to the syrup. Cover and leave to steep for 30 minutes. Strain the syrup through a fine-mesh sieve into an airtight container and discard the solids. The syrup will keep for up to 1 month in the refrigerator, but the flavour is strongest in the first 2 days.

Put the citrus syrup and smoked rosemary in a sterilised 1 litre (34 fl oz) glass jar or bottle and pour over the rum. Seal the jar tightly and store in a cool, dark place for 3 days, gently shaking the jar occasionally to infuse the flavours.

After 3 days, strain the rum through a fine-mesh sieve into a large jug, and discard the rosemary. Strain again through a fine-mesh sieve lined with a muslin (cheesecloth) or a coffee filter. Transfer to one large or several smaller sterilised glass bottles and seal tightly.

COCKTAIL TIP

Serve a single measure (25 ml/¾ fl oz) infused rum over ice in a rocks glass, garnished with a charred rosemary sprig.

PINE VODKA

Makes
800 ml (27 fl oz)

Takes
50 minutes,
*   plus 3–4 days to infuse*

Ingredients
2 Spruce Pine tops
*   or Douglas fir tops*
100 ml (3½ fl oz) Pine Syrup
*   (see below)*
700 ml (23½ fl oz)
*   unflavoured vodka*

Pine Syrup
1 handful Spruce Pine
*   or Douglas fir tops,*
*   roughly chopped*
250 g (9 oz/1¼ cups)
*   granulated sugar*

With its fresh and resinated flavour, making pine syrup first is the best way to capture the taste for this infusion. Pine needles can be used for tea, but adding them to alcohol makes a perfect base for cocktails in the festive season.

To make the Pine Syrup, put the pine tops in a heatproof bowl and pour over 250 ml (8½ fl oz) boiling water. Cover and leave to steep for at least 30 minutes, or up to 24 hours. Strain through a fine-mesh sieve into a saucepan, discarding the solids. Set the pan over medium–low heat and add the sugar. Bring to a simmer, stirring until the sugar has dissolved. Simmer for a further minute, then remove from the heat and set aside to cool. Store in an airtight container in the refrigerator for up to 1 month.

Put the pine tops and Pine Syrup in a sterilised 1 litre (34 fl oz) glass jar or bottle and pour over the vodka. Seal the jar tightly and store in a cool, dark place for 3 days, gently shaking the jar occasionally to help infuse the flavours.

After 3 days, strain the vodka through a fine-mesh sieve into a large jug, and discard the pine. Strain again through a fine-mesh sieve lined with a muslin (cheesecloth) or a coffee filter. Transfer to one large or several smaller sterilised glass bottles, add a pine sprig, and seal tightly.

COCKTAIL TIP

For an Alpine Rocks, add a single measure of infused vodka to a cocktail shaker with ice. Shake briefly, then strain into a chilled cocktail glass and garnish with an olive and a pine sprig.

JUNIPER AND VANILLA GIN

Makes
700 ml (23½ fl oz)

Takes
10 minutes,
    plus 3 days to infuse

Ingredients
2 tablespoons juniper berries
1 vanilla pod, split lengthways
    and seeds scraped
700 ml (23½ fl oz) gin

Juniper berries have been used to flavour gin since the 17th century. This infusion further enhances the juniper flavour, which is sharp with a resinated hint of citrus. Adding vanilla pods gives a slightly sweet, smokey taste which gently rounds this infusion into a great, boozy base.

Put the juniper berries and vanilla pod and seeds in a sterilised 1 litre (34 fl oz) glass jar or bottle and pour over the gin. Seal the jar tightly and store in a cool, dark place for 3 days, gently shaking the jar occasionally to help infuse the flavours.

After 3 days, strain the gin through a fine-mesh sieve into a large jug, and discard the solids. Strain again through a fine-mesh sieve lined with a muslin (cheesecloth) or a coffee filter. Transfer to one large or several smaller sterilised glass bottles and seal tightly.

COCKTAIL TIPS

For a Juniper Mule, mix 2 measures (50 ml/1¾ fl oz) infused gin with 200 ml (7 fl oz) ginger beer and 2–3 dashes Angostura bitters in a highball glass.

To make an Apple and Juniper Fizz, mix a single measure (25 ml/¾ fl oz) infused gin with 1 tablespoon Honey Syrup (p. 62) and 150 ml (5 fl oz) Appletiser or sparkling apple juice. Pour into a cocktail glass and sprinkle with vanilla powder to garnish.

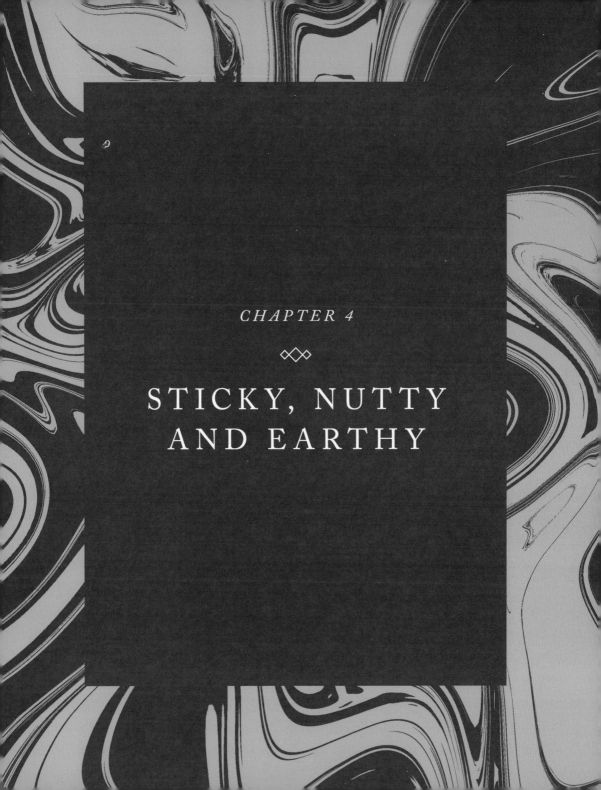

CHAPTER 4

◇◇◇

STICKY, NUTTY AND EARTHY

HONEYCOMB-INFUSED DARK RUM

Makes
700 ml (23½ fl oz)

Takes
10 minutes,
*   plus 3 days to infuse*

Ingredients
1 honeycomb, cut in half
700 ml (23½ fl oz) dark rum

Honey is truly the nectar of the gods. Honey left in its honeycomb is the purest, rawest form, while the wax also has nutritional and health benefits. Using the whole honeycomb to infuse this rum looks so beautiful with its glowing colour, and also makes it a perfect, impressive gift.

Put the honeycomb in a sterilised 1 litre (34 fl oz) glass jar or bottle and pour over the rum. Seal the jar tightly and store in a cool, dark place for 3 days, gently shaking the jar occasionally to help infuse the flavours.

Transfer to one large or several smaller sterilised glass bottles and seal tightly. If you plan to store the rum for more than 3–4 days, remove the honeycomb. Alternatively, leave the honeycomb in the bottle and serve straight out as a showstopper!

COCKTAIL TIPS

To make a Canchànchara, mix a single measure (25 ml/¾ fl oz) infused rum with the juice of 1 lime and build over ice in a rocks glass.

For a Pomrum, add 2 measures (50 ml/1¾ fl oz) infused rum to a cocktail shaker with 100 ml (3½ fl oz) pomegranate juice, 50 ml (1¾ fl oz) orange juice and 1 teaspoon Honey Syrup (p. 62). Top with ice and shake well, then strain into a cocktail glass and garnish with an orange slice.

LIQUORICE WHISKEY

Makes
700 ml (23½ fl oz)

Takes
10 minutes,
*   plus 3 days to infuse*

Ingredients
2 liquorice sticks
1 tablespoon Simple Syrup
*   (p. 127)*
700 ml (23½ fl oz) whiskey

Sourcing good quality liquorice sticks from specialist suppliers produces the best flavour. Its bittersweet, anise-like flavour is really warming and pairs well with whiskey.

Put the liquorice sticks and simple syrup in a sterilised 1 litre (34 fl oz) glass jar or bottle and pour over the whiskey. Seal the jar tightly and store in a cool, dark place for 3 days, gently shaking the jar occasionally to help infuse the flavours.

After 3 days, strain the whiskey through a fine-mesh sieve into a large jug, and discard the liquorice. Strain again through a fine-mesh sieve lined with a muslin (cheesecloth) or a coffee filter. Transfer to one large or several smaller sterilised glass bottles and seal tightly. If you give this as a gift, fasten a liquorice stick to the bottle with a gift tag.

COCKTAIL TIPS

Serve a single measure (25 ml/¾ fl oz) infused whiskey over ice in a glass, garnished with a liquorice stick.

For a take on the Liquorice Stick cocktail, top a single measure of infused whiskey with cola in a highball glass and garnish with a piece of liquorice and cacao nibs.

TONKA BEAN BRANDY

Makes
700 ml (23½ fl oz)

Takes
10 minutes,
    plus 3 days to infuse

Ingredients
4 tonka beans
1 tablespoon Simple Syrup
    (p. 127)
700 ml (23½ fl oz) brandy

Tonka beans come from a South American flowering tree and have a taste that is similar to vanilla, but with fruity and spicy, as opposed to floral, elements to its flavour. This infusion of brandy is delicious served with an accompaniment of dates to nibble, which really bring out its subtle flavours.

Put the tonka beans and simple syrup in a sterilised 1 litre (34 fl oz) glass jar or bottle and pour over the brandy. Seal the jar tightly and store in a cool, dark place for 3 days, gently shaking the jar occasionally to help infuse the flavours.

After 3 days, strain the brandy through a fine-mesh sieve into a large jug, and discard the beans. Strain again through a fine-mesh sieve lined with a muslin (cheesecloth) or a coffee filter. Transfer to one large or several smaller sterilised glass bottles and seal tightly.

COCKTAIL TIPS

For a riff on an Espresso Martini, mix a single measure (25 ml/¾ fl oz) infused brandy with 25 ml (¾ fl oz) Tia Maria, 25 ml (¾ fl oz) espresso and 1 teaspoon vanilla extract. Pour into a martini glass and garnish with coffee beans.

Add a single measure of infused brandy and 1 teaspoon honey to a cocktail shaker with ice. Shake briefly, then strain into a chilled cocktail glass and serve with dates on the side.

CHOCOLATE BOURBON

Makes
700 ml (23½ fl oz)

Takes
*10 minutes,
    plus 3 days to infuse*

Ingredients
*100 g (3½ oz) cacao nibs
1 tablespoon maple syrup
1 vanilla pod, split lengthways
    and seeds scraped
3 cardamom pods,
    bruised (optional)
700 ml (23½ fl oz) bourbon*

Chocolate Bourbon comes from infusing bourbon with cacao and it makes the perfect affogato. Traditionally, Italians pour a shot of coffee over ice cream, to make a creamy coffee dessert but I like to use salted caramel ice cream, a shot of coffee and a shot of chocolate bourbon. Salty, sweet, boozy and chocolatey, all at once.

Put the cacao nibs, maple syrup, vanilla pod and seeds and cardamom pods, if using, in a sterilised 1 litre (34 fl oz) glass jar or bottle and pour over the bourbon. Seal the jar tightly and store in a cool, dark place for 3 days, gently shaking the jar occasionally to help infuse the flavours.

After 3 days, strain the bourbon through a fine-mesh sieve into a large jug, and discard the nibs and spices. Strain again through a fine-mesh sieve lined with a muslin (cheesecloth) or a coffee filter. Transfer to one large or several smaller sterilised glass bottles and seal tightly.

COCKTAIL TIPS

For a Spiked Salted-Caramel Affogato, serve salted-caramel ice cream in a bowl or a serving glass with a shot of espresso and a shot of Chocolate Bourbon on the side for pouring over.

To make a Cherry Chocolate Cocktail, mix 2 measures (50 ml/1¾ fl oz) infused bourbon with 50 ml (1¾ fl oz) Cherry Syrup (p. 38) and 1–2 dashes Angostura bitters. Serve in a cocktail glass, garnished with a fresh cherry.

TROPICAL RUM

Makes
800 ml (27 fl oz)

Takes
10 minutes,
*   plus 6 days to infuse*

Ingredients
200 g (7 oz) mixed tropical
*   fruit (e.g. guava, dragon*
*   fruit (pitiya), mangosteen*
*   and lychees)*
100 ml (3½ fl oz) tinned
*   lychee syrup or Lychee*
*   Syrup (p. 127)*
2 limes, quartered
700 ml (23½ fl oz) rum
½ grapefruit

Tuti-tropical-frutti, use whatever tropical fruit you have access to – the sweeter the better. This is great served topped with coconut water and garnished with tropical fruit.

Put the mixed fruit and lychee syrup in a sterilised 1 litre (34 fl oz) glass jar or bottle and pour over the rum. Seal the jar tightly and store in a cool, dark place for 3 days, gently shaking the jar occasionally to help infuse the flavours.

After 3 days, peel the lime zest with a potato peeler and remove the pith. Cut the zest into thin strips. Slice the grapefruit flesh. Add the zest and flesh to the rum, stirring to disperse. Seal and store for a further 3 days, to allow the rum to absorb the flavours.

Strain the rum through a fine-mesh sieve into a large jug and discard the fruit and zest. Strain again through a fine-mesh sieve lined with a muslin (cheesecloth) or a coffee filter. Transfer to one large or several smaller sterilised glass bottles and seal tightly.

COCKTAIL TIP

To make a Tropical Fruit Rum Jug, combine 200 ml (7 fl oz) infused rum with 200 ml (7 fl oz) coconut water in a jug. Add 200 g (7 oz) mixed tropical fruits, such as mangosteen, dragon fruit (pitiya), lychees or passion fruit, then add some ice and mix well.

CINNAMON AND NUTMEG DARK RUM

Makes
900 ml (30½ fl oz)

Takes
10 minutes,
    plus 3 days to infuse

Ingredients
2 nutmegs: 1 grated and 1 whole
4 tablespoons maple syrup
3 cinnamon sticks
900 ml (30½ fl oz) dark rum

Cinnamon is extremely aromatic and both sweet and savoury at the same time. Nutmeg has a warming, deep flavour with hints of clove. Both are classic spices that pair extremely well with rum. I particularly love drinking this rum hot and buttered, on a cold day sitting next to a roaring fire.

Put the nutmegs, maple syrup and cinnamon sticks in a sterilised 1 litre (34 fl oz) glass jar or bottle and pour over the dark rum. Seal the jar tightly and store in a cool, dark place for 3 days, gently shaking the jar occasionally to help infuse the flavours.

After 3 days, strain the rum through a fine-mesh sieve into a large jug, and discard the spices. Strain again through a fine-mesh sieve lined with a muslin (cheesecloth) or a coffee filter. Transfer to one large or several smaller sterilised glass bottles and seal tightly.

COCKTAIL TIPS

Mix a single measure (25 ml/¾ fl oz) infused rum with 1 teaspoon Simple Syrup (p. 127), a grating of fresh nutmeg and 1 cinnamon stick for the traditional cocktail, Bumbo.

For a Hot Buttered Rum, serve a single measure of infused rum hot with 2 teaspoons butter, 2 teaspoons honey and 1 cinnamon stick.

WALNUT COGNAC

Makes

1 litre (34 fl oz)

Takes

15 minutes,
   plus 3 days to infuse

Ingredients

200 g (7 oz/1⅓ cups) walnuts
500 ml (17 fl oz) Benedictine
500 ml (17 fl oz) Cognac

Walnuts, unlike other nuts, have a mild taste but also have sharp and tangy notes. Make sure that you use the freshest walnuts as they have a tendency to become rancid. The addition of Benedictine (a sweet, herbal liqueur) to the cognac and walnuts, enhances the subtle flavours of this mix.

Toast the walnuts in a frying pan over medium–low heat, until lightly brown. Leave to cool, then transfer them to a sterilised 1 litre (34 fl oz) glass jar or bottle and pour over the Benedictine and Cognac. Seal the jar tightly and store in a cool, dark place for 3 days, gently shaking the jar occasionally to help infuse the flavours.

After 3 days, strain the liquid through a fine-mesh sieve into a large jug, and discard the walnuts. Strain again through a fine-mesh sieve lined with a muslin (cheesecloth) or a coffee filter. Transfer to one large or several smaller sterilised glass bottles and seal tightly.

COCKTAIL TIP

Make a Maple Walnut by mixing 2 measures (50 ml/1¾ fl oz) Walnut Cognac with 3 dashes Angostura bitters. Serve in a rocks glass over ice.

HOMEMADE AMARETTO

Makes
850 ml (28½ fl oz)

Takes
30 minutes,
 plus 3 days to infuse

Ingredients
200 g (7 oz/1 cup) dark brown
 sugar
1–2 tablespoons natural almond
 extract (to taste)
2 teaspoons natural vanilla extract
600 ml (20½ fl oz)
 unflavoured vodka
155 g (5½ oz/1 cup) almonds

This infusion is so uncomplicated yet surprising. I love to serve it alongside chocolate truffles to contrast the tastes.

Combine 250 ml (8½ fl oz) water and the sugar in a heavy-based saucepan over medium heat and simmer gently, until the sugar has dissolved. Remove from the heat and leave to cool for 15 minutes. Add the almond and vanilla extracts, vodka and almonds to the saucepan, and mix to combine.

Pour the amaretto into a sterilised 1 litre (34 fl oz) glass jar or bottle. Seal the jar tightly and store in a cool, dark place for 3 days, gently shaking the jar occasionally to help infuse the flavours.

Strain the amaretto through a fine-mesh sieve into a large jug and discard the nuts. Strain again through a fine-mesh sieve lined with a muslin (cheesecloth) or a coffee filter. Transfer to one large or several smaller sterilised glass bottles and seal tightly.

COCKTAIL TIPS

For a Morning After, add a single measure (25 ml/¾ fl oz) Homemade Amaretto, 25 ml (¾ fl oz) green chartreuse, 2 teaspoons dark rum and 1 teaspoon Simple Syrup (p. 127) to 100 ml (3½ fl oz) hot black coffee. Serve in a mug.

Alternatively, serve a single measure of infused vodka in a liqueur glass with chocolate truffles on the side.

PISTACHIO GIN

Makes
750 ml (25½ fl oz)

Takes
10 minutes,
*   plus 3 days to infuse*

Ingredients
200 g (7 oz/1⅓ cups)
*   pistachio nuts, shelled*
1 vanilla pod, split lengthways
*   and seeds scraped*
1 teaspoon edible dried rose petals
60 ml (2 fl oz) Simple Syrup
*   (p. 127)*
700 ml (23½ fl oz) gin

This Pistachio Gin infusion has a gentle vanilla, rose and nutty flavour. It's delicate and light and works perfectly as a Pistachio Rose Mule.

Put the pistachio nuts, vanilla pod and seeds, edible rose petals and simple syrup into a sterilised 1 litre (34 fl oz) glass jar or bottle and pour over the gin. Seal the jar tightly and store in a cool, dark place for 3 days, gently shaking the jar occasionally to help infuse the flavours.

After 3 days, strain the gin through a fine-mesh sieve into a large jug, and discard the solids. Strain again through a fine-mesh sieve lined with a muslin (cheesecloth) or a coffee filter. Transfer to one large or several smaller sterilised glass bottles and seal tightly.

COCKTAIL TIP

For a Pistachio Rose Mule, combine 2 measures (50 ml/1¾ fl oz) infused gin, the juice of ½ lime and 1 teaspoon Ginger Syrup (p. 127) in a highball glass. Top with 150 ml (5 fl oz) ginger beer and garnish with edible rose petals. Serve some pistachio nuts in a bowl on the side.

HAZELNUT LIQUEUR

Makes

700 ml (23½ fl oz)

Takes

10 minutes,
*   plus approx. 3 weeks to infuse*

Ingredients

100 g (3½ oz/½ cup) dark
*   brown sugar*
1 vanilla pod, split lengthways
*   and seeds scraped*
300 g (10½ oz/2¼ cups) raw
hazelnuts
*   with skin, roughly chopped*
300 ml (10 fl oz)
*   unflavoured vodka*
250 ml (8½ fl oz) brandy

Hazlenuts have a uniquely sweet and buttery flavour. Combined with vanilla, sugar, vodka and brandy, a lovely liqueur is created – all in your own home.

Heat the sugar and 150 ml (5 fl oz) water in a small saucepan over medium heat, until the sugar has dissolved. Remove from the heat and leave to cool. Allow to steep for 3 days, shaking occasionally. Add the vanilla pod and seeds and leave to steep for a further 3–5 days.

Put the hazelnuts, vodka, brandy and sugar mixture in a sterilised 1 litre (34 fl oz) glass jar or bottle and mix well. Store at room temperature for 2 weeks, gently shaking the jar occasionally to help infuse the flavours. Sample often to test the flavour. Once you are happy with it, strain the liquid through a fine-mesh sieve into a jug, and discard the hazelnuts and vanilla pod. Strain again through a fine-mesh sieve lined with a muslin (cheesecloth) or a coffee filter. Transfer to one large or several smaller sterilised glass bottles and seal tightly. Refrigerate for up to 2 months.

COCKTAIL TIP

To make Hazelnut Cider, combine a single measure (25 ml/¾ fl oz) Hazelnut Liqueur in a cocktail shaker with 50 ml (1¾ fl oz) apple cider, 1½ teaspoons Honey Syrup (p. 62) and ice. Add a dash of Angostura bitters, shake briefly, then strain into a chilled highball glass over ice.

BEETROOT AND SOUR CHERRY VODKA

Makes
700 ml (23½ fl oz)

Takes
10 minutes,
*   plus 3 days to infuse*

Ingredients
3 beetroot (beets), scrubbed
*   and quartered*
200 g (7 oz/1½ cups) dried
*   sour cherries*
700 ml (23½ fl oz)
*   unflavoured vodka*

The earthiness of beetroot and the tart sweetness of dried, sour cherries work really well together. This is an unusual infusion but looks so pretty in a champagne saucer, garnished with a slice of candied beetroot.

Put the beetroot and sour cherries in a sterilised 1 litre (34 fl oz) glass jar or bottle and pour over the vodka. Seal the jar tightly and store in a cool, dark place for 3 days, until the colour has deepened. Gently shake the jar occasionally to help infuse the flavours.

After 3 days, strain the vodka through a fine-mesh sieve into a large jug, and discard the solids. Strain again through a fine-mesh sieve lined with a muslin (cheesecloth) or a coffee filter. Transfer to one large or several smaller sterilised glass bottles and seal tightly.

COCKTAIL TIP

For a Beet Jax, mix 2 measures (50 ml/1¾ fl oz) infused vodka with 25 ml (¾ fl oz) red vermouth, 1 teaspoon Simple Syrup (p. 127) and the juice of ½ lime in a cocktail shaker with ice. Shake briefly, strain into a chilled cocktail glass and garnish with a thin slice of fresh beetroot.

SAFFRON GIN

Makes
700 ml (23½ fl oz)

Takes
10 minutes,
    plus 3 days to infuse

Ingredients
10 g (⅓ oz) saffron threads
100 ml (3½ fl oz)
    Simple Syrup (p. 127)
600 ml (20½ fl oz) gin

Saffron is spicy and pungent with a slightly bitter flavour and strong aroma. Infused in gin, it also adds vibrant colour and makes a good looking, gin-based cocktail.

Put the saffron and Simple Syrup in a sterilised 1 litre (34 fl oz) glass jar or bottle and pour over the gin. Seal the jar tightly and store in a cool, dark place for 3 days, until the colour has deepened. Gently shake the jar occasionally to help infuse the flavours.

After 3 days, strain the gin through a fine-mesh sieve into a large jug, and discard the saffron. Strain again through a fine-mesh sieve lined with a muslin (cheesecloth) or a coffee filter. Transfer to one large or several smaller sterilised glass bottles and seal tightly.

COCKTAIL TIPS

To make a Saffron Cooler, combine 300 ml (10 fl oz) Saffron Gin with 200 ml (7 fl oz) fino sherry and ½ chopped rockmelon (cantaloupe) in a large jug. Top up with soda water and ice, and serve.

Add the juice of 1 lemon and some smashed cardamom pods to 1 quantity Saffron gin and top with lemonade for Spiked Saffron Lemonade.

ANGELICA AND ORRIS ROOT GIN

Makes
650 ml (22 fl oz)

Takes
10 minutes,
*   plus 3 days to infuse*

Ingredients
50 g (1¾ oz) Angelica root
2 tablespoons coriander seeds
1 tablespoon juniper berries
1 teaspoon orris root powder
*   (optional)*
650 ml (22 fl oz) gin

Angelica and orris root are usually combined as part of the base mixture of spices for gin. They are very much background spices, though, but in this infusion their flavours have been ramped up a little to delicious effect. Specialist stores sell both, but make sure it's food grade.

Put the Angelica root, coriander seeds, juniper berries and orris root powder, if using, in a sterilised 1 litre (34 fl oz) glass jar or bottle and pour over the gin. Seal the jar tightly and store in a cool, dark place for 3 days, gently shaking the jar occasionally to help infuse the flavours.

After 3 days, strain the gin through a fine-mesh sieve into a large jug, and discard the spices. Strain again through a fine-mesh sieve lined with a muslin (cheesecloth) or a coffee filter. Transfer to one large or several smaller sterilised glass bottles and seal tightly.

COCKTAIL TIP

Make a Queen Victoria's Tonic by adding 25 ml (¾ fl oz) elderflower liqueur to 2 measures (50 ml/1¾ fl oz) infused gin in a highball glass. Top up with soda water and garnish with some lemongrass.

TURMERIC AND PICKLED DILL CUCUMBER VODKA

Makes
650 ml (22 fl oz)

Takes
10 minutes,
*   plus 3 days to infuse*

Ingredients
100 g (3½ oz) pickled dill
*   cucumbers*
1–2 fresh turmeric roots, peeled
600 ml (20½ fl oz)
*   unflavoured vodka*
50 ml (1¾ fl oz)
*   Simple Syrup (p. 127)*

The colour of this infusion is just glorious. This is also one of those recipes that you sweeten to your own taste. And eating the pickles after they've finished infusing the booze is one of my favourite things to do!

Put the pickled cucumbers and turmeric roots in a sterilised 1 litre (34 fl oz) glass jar or bottle and pour over the vodka and simple syrup. Seal the jar tightly and store in a cool, dark place for 3 days, until the colour has deepened. Gently shake the jar occasionally to help infuse the flavours.

After 3 days, strain the vodka through a fine-mesh sieve into a large jug, and discard the solids. Strain again through a fine-mesh sieve lined with a muslin (cheesecloth) or a coffee filter. Transfer to one large or several smaller sterilised glass bottles and seal tightly.

COCKTAIL TIPS

For a Dirty Martini, add 100 ml (3½ fl oz) infused vodka and 25 ml (¾ fl oz) dry vermouth to a cocktail shaker with ice. Shake briefly, then strain into a chilled martini glass. Garnish with a slice of dill pickle.

Make a Dirty Watermelon and Cucumber Juice by mixing 200 ml (7 fl oz) fresh watermelon and cucumber juice with 2 measures (50 ml/1¾ fl oz) infused vodka. Serve over ice in a highball glass.

CHAPTER 5

◇◇◇

HOT AND SPICY

PINK PEPPERCORN
AND PINEAPPLE TEQUILA

Makes

600 ml (20½ fl oz)

Takes

10 minutes,
*   plus 3 days to infuse*

Ingredients

1 pineapple, skin removed and
*   flesh cut into half-rounds*
2–3 tablespoons pink peppercorns
600 ml (20½ fl oz) tequila

Apart from being so pretty in its infusing process, this is one of those layered flavours that initially tastes like boozy pineapple and then you get the lighter, sweet–sharp peppery taste of the pink peppercorns just a little in the background.

Put the pineapple and pink peppercorns in a sterilised 1 litre (34 fl oz) glass jar or bottle and pour over the tequila. Seal the jar tightly and store in a cool, dark place for 3 days, gently shaking the jar occasionally to help infuse the flavours.

After 3 days, strain the tequila through a fine-mesh sieve into a large jug, and discard the fruit and peppercorns. Strain again through a fine-mesh sieve lined with a muslin (cheesecloth) or a coffee filter. Transfer to one large or several smaller sterilised glass bottles and seal tightly.

COCKTAIL TIP

To make a Pineapple Margarita, muddle some pineapple and mint in the bottom of a cocktail shaker. Add 2 measures (50 ml/1¾ fl oz) infused tequila, 25 ml (¾ fl oz) triple sec and some ice, then shake briefly. Rub pineapple juice around the rim of a chilled cocktail glass and dip it in salt. Strain the pineapple margarita into the glass and serve, garnished with a pineapple wedge.

HORSERADISH, RASPBERRY AND PEACH VODKA

Makes
600 ml (20½ fl oz)

Takes
10 minutes,
    plus 3 days to infuse

Ingredients
2 peaches, cut into wedges
5 cm (2 in) piece horseradish,
    peeled and grated
100 g (3½ oz/1 cup) raspberries
600 ml (20½ fl oz)
    unflavoured vodka

Horseradish has a sharp, mustard-like flavour, but shouldn't just be limited to roast beef. Paired with peach and raspberry in this infusion it adds a tart, light freshness that enhances the sweetness of the fruit. This is a super-refreshing tipple.

Combine the peach wedges, raspberries and grated horseradish in a sterilised 1 litre (34 fl oz) glass jar or bottle and pour over the vodka. Seal the jar tightly and store in a cool, dark place for 3 days, until the colour has deepened. Gently shake the jar occasionally to help infuse the flavours.

After 3 days, strain the vodka through a fine-mesh sieve into a large jug, and discard the solids. Strain again through a fine-mesh sieve lined with a muslin (cheesecloth) or a coffee filter. Transfer to one large or several smaller sterilised glass bottles and seal tightly.

COCKTAIL TIP

Serve a single measure (25 ml/¾ fl oz) infused vodka in a large wine glass over ice, topped with soda water and garnished with sliced peaches, whole raspberries and julienned horseradish.

WASABI, GINGER AND CUCUMBER GIN

Makes
600 ml (20½ fl oz)

Takes
10 minutes,
*   plus 3 days to infuse*

Ingredients
2 cucumbers, thinly sliced
*   into rounds*
2 teaspoons wasabi powder
20 g (¾ oz) pickled ginger
600 ml (20½ fl oz) gin

Wasabi is a Japanese type of horseradish with a powerful kick. Paired with ginger and cucumber this infusion is fiery and cool at the same time. A perfect accompaniment to sushi.

Put the cucumbers, wasabi powder and ginger in a sterilised 1 litre (34 fl oz) glass jar or bottle and pour over the gin. Seal the jar tightly and store in a cool, dark place for 3 days, until the colour has deepened. Gently shake the jar occasionally to help infuse the flavours.

After 3 days, strain the gin through a fine-mesh sieve into a large jug, and discard the solids. Strain again through a fine-mesh sieve lined with a muslin (cheesecloth) or a coffee filter. Transfer to one large or several smaller sterilised glass bottles and seal tightly.

COCKTAIL TIP

To make a Wasabi Spice, combine 2 measures (50 ml/1¾ fl oz) infused gin with 20 ml (¾ fl oz) Ginger Syrup (p. 127), ½ sliced cucumber and 1 sprig of mint in a highball glass. Add some ice and top up with soda water.

STAR ANISE AND MAPLE BOURBON

Makes
700 ml (23½ fl oz)

Takes
10 minutes,
*   plus 3 days to infuse*

Ingredients
6 star anise
3 cloves
1 cinnamon stick
100 ml (3½ fl oz) maple syrup
600 ml (20½ fl oz) bourbon

Spicy, warm, sweet and fragrant, all at once. This flavoured bourbon is delicious as a cocktail base, or just as nice over ice.

Put the star anise, cloves, cinnamon stick and maple syrup in a sterilised 1 litre (34 fl oz) glass jar or bottle and pour over the bourbon. Seal the jar tightly and store in a cool, dark place for 3 days, gently shaking the jar occasionally to help infuse the flavours.

After 3 days, strain the bourbon through a fine-mesh sieve into a large jug, and discard the spices. Strain again through a fine-mesh sieve lined with a muslin (cheesecloth) or a coffee filter. Transfer to one large or several smaller sterilised glass bottles and seal tightly.

COCKTAIL TIP

Add 2 teaspoons Tea Syrup (p. 127) and the juice of ½ lemon to a single measure (25 ml/¾ fl oz) infused bourbon for a Chai Bourbon Sour.

SMOKY ANCHO CHILLI AND GRAPEFRUIT RUM

Makes
600 ml (20 fl oz)

Takes
10 minutes,
*   plus 3 days to infuse*

Ingredients
1 large dried ancho chilli
1 grapefruit, sliced
600 ml (20½ fl oz) rum

The smoky, earthy heat of the ancho chilli combines well with the zing of grapefruit citrus to produce this infusion.

Put the ancho chilli and sliced grapefruit in a sterilised 1 litre (34 fl oz) glass jar or bottle and pour over the rum. Seal the jar tightly and store in a cool, dark place for 3 days, gently shaking the jar occasionally to help infuse the flavours. It is important to taste the rum regularly to test the heat and decide when you think it's ready. The longer you leave it, the hotter it will become.

After 3 days, strain the rum through a fine-mesh sieve into a large jug, and discard the solids. Strain again through a fine-mesh sieve lined with a muslin (cheesecloth) or a coffee filter. Transfer to one large or several smaller sterilised glass bottles and seal tightly.

COCKTAIL TIP

Make a Spicy Grapefruit and Chipotle Cocktail by building 2 measures (50 ml/1¾ fl oz) infused rum, 25 ml (¾ fl oz) Grand Marnier and 150 ml (5 fl oz) grapefruit juice over ice in a rocks glass.

JALAPEÑO VODKA

Makes
700 ml (23½ fl oz)

Takes
10 minutes,
    plus 3 days to infuse

Ingredients
3 jalapeño chillies, halved
100 ml (3½ fl oz)
    Simple Syrup (p. 127)
600 ml (20½ fl oz)
    unflavoured vodka

In the chilli family, the jalapeno is one of mild to medium heat. This vodka infusion is so delicious just served over ice, but is also great with some added sweetness – the best cocktails have a balance of booze, sour, sweet and heat.

Put the jalapeños and simple syrup in a sterilised 1 litre (34 fl oz) glass jar or bottle and pour over the vodka. Seal the jar tightly and store in a cool, dark place for 3 days, gently shaking the jar occasionally to help infuse the flavours.

After 3 days, strain the vodka through a fine-mesh sieve into a large jug, and discard the the chillies. Strain again through a fine-mesh sieve lined with a muslin (cheesecloth) or a coffee filter. Transfer to one large or several smaller sterilised glass bottles and seal tightly.

COCKTAIL TIP

To make a Jalapeño Daisy, combine a single measure (25 ml/ ¾ fl oz) infused vodka with 1 tablespoon yuzu juice and 1 teaspoon Simple Syrup (p. 127) in a cocktail shaker and top with ice. Shake briefly and strain into a chilled cocktail glass.

RED CHILLI AND PASSION FRUIT MEZCAL

Makes

600 ml (20½ fl oz)

Takes

10 minutes,
*   plus up to 3 days to infuse*

Ingredients

4–5 red chillies, halved
4 passion fruit , halved
*   and pulp scooped out*
600 ml (20½ fl oz) mezcal

Mezcal is a cousin to tequila. It's made from roasting agave over flaming hot volcanic rock, from where it gets its earthy and smoky flavour. Infused with red chillis and passion fruit, this mezcal really is a taste sensation.

Place the chillies and passion fruit pulp in a sterilised 1 litre (34 fl oz) glass jar or bottle and pour over the mezcal. Seal the jar tightly and store in the refrigerator for 3 days, gently shaking the jar occasionally to help infuse the flavours. It is important to taste the mezcal regularly to test the heat and decide when you think it's ready. The longer you leave it, the hotter it will become.

After 3 days, depending on how hot you like it, strain the mezcal through a fine-mesh sieve into a large jug, and discard the solids. Strain again through a fine-mesh sieve lined with a muslin (cheesecloth) or a coffee filter. Transfer to one large or several smaller sterilised glass bottles and seal tightly.

COCKTAIL TIP

Combine 70 ml (2¼ fl oz) infused mezcal, the juice of 1 lime,
1 tablespoon hibiscus syrup (available at specialist food stores)
and 200 ml (7 fl oz) ginger beer for a Don Diabolo.

CAYENNE PEPPER AND AGAVE TEQUILA

Makes

700 ml (23½ fl oz)

Takes

10 minutes,
*   plus 3 days to infuse*

Ingredients

1 teaspoon cayenne pepper
100 ml (3½ fl oz) agave syrup
600 ml (20½ fl oz) tequila

It's the cayenne pepper that adds both heat and bite to this tequila, along with spicey and bay-like notes. Keep checking as you make this infusion to be sure it suits your heat levels, because it's all about personal taste.

Combine the cayenne pepper and agave in a sterilised 1 litre (34 fl oz) glass jar or bottle and pour over the tequila. Seal the jar tightly and store in a cool, dark place for approximately 3 days.

There is no need to strain the tequila. Use straight away.

COCKTAIL TIP

For a Mango Hot Mama, combine 2 measures (50 ml/1¾ fl oz) infused tequila with 25 ml (¾ fl oz) coconut rum. Blitz ⅓ mango (stone removed) to a purée in a food processor. Add a handful of ice and pulse again until the ice has broken into shards. Rub the rim of a cocktail glass with lime juice and dip in a mixture of 1-part sugar, 1-part salt and a sprinkling of cayenne pepper, or simply serve with some ice, a dash of soda water and a wedge of watermelon.

BLACK PEPPERCORN
AND STRAWBERRY VODKA

Makes
650 ml (22 fl oz)

Takes
10 minutes,
plus 3 days to infuse

Ingredients
3 teaspoons black peppercorns
300 g (10½ oz/2 cups)
strawberries, hulled and sliced
50 ml (1¾ fl oz)
Simple Syrup (p. 127)
600 ml (20½ fl oz)
unflavoured vodka

This infusion of black pepper and strawberries is so special. It's sweet and hot and, when served on ice with some strawberries and edible flowers for decoration, it's just plain pretty. Pretty with a bite...

Combine the black peppercorns, strawberries and simple syrup in a sterilised 1 litre (34 fl oz) glass jar or bottle and pour over the vodka. Seal the jar tightly and store in a cool, dark place for 3 days, until the colour has deepened. Gently shake the jar occasionally to help infuse the flavours.

After 3 days, strain the vodka through a fine-mesh sieve into a large jug, and discard the fruit and peppercorns. Strain again through a fine-mesh sieve lined with a muslin (cheesecloth) or a coffee filter. Transfer to one large or several smaller sterilised glass bottles and seal tightly.

COCKTAIL TIP

Simply serve a single measure (25 ml/¾ fl oz) infused vodka in a rocks glass over ice. Garnish with edible flowers and strawberries for an extra touch.

123

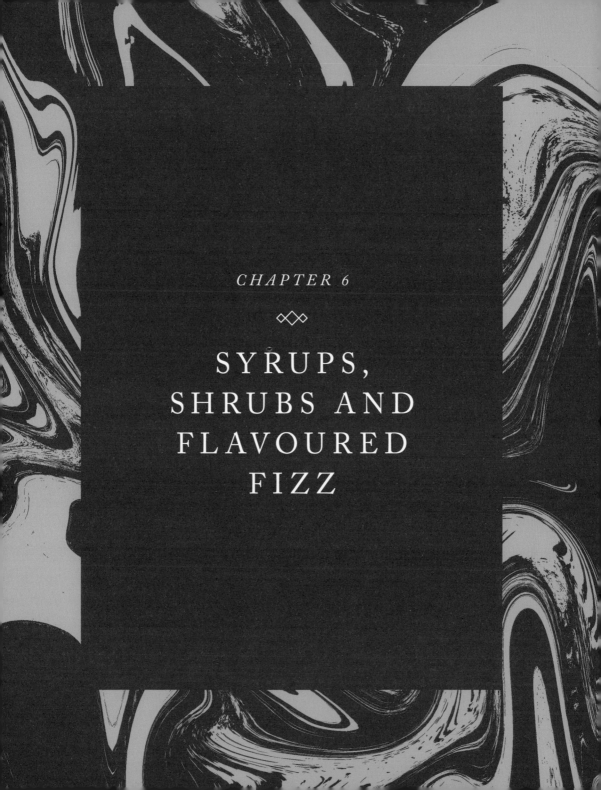

CHAPTER 6

✧✧✧

SYRUPS, SHRUBS AND FLAVOURED FIZZ

SIMPLE SYRUP

Makes: *250 ml (8½ fl oz)*
Takes: *10 minutes*

250 ml (8½ fl oz) boiling water
100 g (3½ oz/generous ½ cup) caster (superfine) sugar

Combine the boiling water and sugar in a small saucepan over medium–high heat and stir until the sugar has dissolved. Remove from the heat and add your choice of flavourings, if using (see tip), or leave plain. Allow to cool completely. Strain the syrup through a fine-mesh sieve into a sterilised 500 ml (17 fl oz) glass jar or bottle, discarding any flavourings. Seal the jar tightly and store in the refrigerator for up to 1 month.

Tip: *You can flavour this syrup with just about anything, including honey, ginger, lychee, green apple, vanilla, or even tea leaves or bags.*

ROSE SYRUP

Makes: *250 ml (8½ fl oz)*
Takes: *10 minutes*

100 g (3½ oz/generous ½ cup) caster (superfine) sugar
1–2 tablespoons rosewater
1 teaspoon dried or fresh edible rose petals

Combine 250 ml (8½ fl oz) boiling water and the sugar in a small saucepan over low heat and stir until the sugar has dissolved. Remove from the heat, add the rosewater and rose petals, and leave to cool completely. Strain the syrup through a fine-mesh sieve into a sterilised 500 ml (17 fl oz) glass jar or bottle, discarding the rose petals. Seal the jar tightly and store in the refrigerator for up to 1 month.

LEMON VERBENA SYRUP

Makes: *250 ml (8½ fl oz)*
Takes: *10 minutes*

100 g (3½ oz/generous ½ cup) caster (superfine) sugar
3 lemon verbena sprigs

Combine 250 ml (8½ fl oz) boiling water and the sugar in a small saucepan over low heat and stir until the sugar has dissolved. Remove from the heat, add the lemon verbena, and leave to cool completely. Strain the syrup through a fine-mesh sieve into a sterilised 500 ml (17 fl oz) glass jar or bottle, discarding the lemon verbena. Seal the jar tightly and store in the refrigerator for 1 week. Remove the lemon verbena sprigs and continue storing for another 3 weeks.

BLACKBERRY AND THYME

Makes: *250 ml (8½ fl oz)*
Takes: *10 minutes*

100 g (3½ oz/generous ½ cup) caster (superfine) sugar
200 g (7 oz/1½ cups) blackberries
5 thyme sprigs

Combine 250 ml (8½ fl oz) boiling water and the sugar in a small saucepan over low heat and stir until the sugar has dissolved. Remove from the heat, add the blackberries and thyme, and leave to cool completely. Strain the syrup through a fine-mesh sieve into a sterilised 500 ml (17 fl oz) glass jar or bottle, discarding the blackberries and thyme. Seal the jar tightly and store in the refrigerator for 1 week.

CHAMOMILE SYRUP

Makes: *250 ml (8½ fl oz)*
Takes: *5 minutes*

100 g (3½ oz/generous ½ cup) caster (superfine) sugar
3 chamomile tea bags

Combine 250 ml (8½ fl oz) boiling water and the
sugar in a small saucepan over low heat and stir
until the sugar has dissolved. Remove from the
heat, add the chamomile tea bags, and leave
to cool completely. Strain the syrup through a
fine-mesh sieve into a sterilised 500 ml (17 fl oz)
glass jar or bottle, discarding the tea bags. Seal
the jar tightly and store in the refrigerator for up
to 1 month.

WHISKEY SYRUP

Makes: *300 ml (10 fl oz)*
Takes: *30 minutes*

100 g (3½ oz/½ cup) light brown sugar
100 ml (3½ fl oz) whiskey
1–2 tablespoons maple syrup

Combine all the ingredients in a small saucepan
with 250 ml (8½ fl oz) boiling water over medium–
high heat. Simmer, whisking occasionally, for
20–25 minutes, until the syrup has thickened.

Strain the syrup through a fine-mesh sieve into a
sterilised 500 ml (17 fl oz) glass jar or bottle. Seal
the jar tightly and store in the refrigerator for up
to 1 month.

PETIMEZI (GRAPE MUST OR GRAPE MOLASSES) SYRUP

Makes: *200 ml (7 fl oz)*
Takes: *1½ hours*

2 kg (4 lb 6 oz) red grapes
2 thyme sprigs (optional)
3 mint leaves (optional)

Crush the grapes in a food mill and extract as much
juice as possible. Discard the solids.

Transfer the grape juice to a fine-mesh sieve
lined with a muslin (cheesecloth) set over a large
saucepan.
Allow to drain thoroughly, pressing down on
the pulp occasionally until all the juice has been
extracted. (This can be done in batches if your sieve
is not large enough to hold all the pulp at once.)

Once it has finished draining, remove the sieve and
bring the grape juice to the boil over medium to
medium–high heat. Cook for about 1 hour, or until
the temperature reaches 112°C (235°F) on a sugar
thermometer. Remove from the heat and leave to
cool completely. The syrup should be dense but
pourable, like honey.

Strain the syrup through a fine-mesh sieve into a
sterilised 500 ml (17 fl oz) glass jar or bottle. Seal
the jar tightly and store in the refrigerator for up
to 1 month.

POMEGRANATE SHRUB

Makes: *750 ml (25½ fl oz)*
Takes: *10 minutes, plus 3 days to infuse*

500 ml (17 fl oz) pomegranate juice
250 ml (8½ fl oz) apple cider vinegar
150 g (5½ oz/1⅓ cups) caster (superfine) sugar
100 g (3½ oz/½ cup) pomegranate seeds

Put all the ingredients in a sterilised 1 litre
(34 fl oz) glass jar or bottle. Seal the jar tightly
and shake vigorously to combine. Store in the
refrigerator to infuse for 3 days before using.
The flavours will continue to mature over time.
Use within 6 months.

APPLE AND FENNEL SHRUB

Makes: *350 ml (12 fl oz)*
Takes: *10 minutes, plus 3 days to infuse*

200 g (7 oz) apple, sliced
200 g (7 oz) fennel, sliced
200 g (7 oz/1 cup) caster (superfine) sugar
350 ml (12 fl oz) apple cider vinegar

Put all the ingredients in a sterilised 1 litre
(34 fl oz) glass jar or bottle. Seal the jar tightly
and shake vigorously to combine. Store in the
refrigerator to infuse for 3 days before using.
Remove the sliced apple and fennel, and use
within 1 week.

CRANBERRY AND CLOVE SHRUB

Makes: *100 ml (3½ fl oz)*
Takes: *10 minutes, plus 3 days to infuse*

300 g (10½ oz/3¼ cups) cranberries
50 g (1¾ oz) raw honey
75 ml (2½ fl oz) apple cider vinegar
8 cloves

Put the cranberries in a sterilised 1 litre (34 fl oz)
glass jar or bottle and lightly crush with a muddler.
Stir in the honey, vinegar and cloves. Store in the
refrigerator to infuse for 3 days, then strain through
a fine-mesh sieve and use straight away.

TANGERINE AND BLACKBERRY FIZZ

Makes: *750 ml (25½ fl oz)*
Takes: *10 minutes, plus overnight to infuse*

2–3 tangerines, halved
150 g (5½ oz/1 generous cup) blackberries
750 ml (25½ fl oz) sparkling water

Simply add the tangerines and blackberries to
the sparkling water and seal in a clean glass jug.
Refrigerate overnight and serve chilled.

GERANIUM FIZZ

Makes: *750 ml (25½ fl oz)*
Takes: *5 minutes*

2 geranium sprigs
2–3 drops orange blossom water
750 ml (25½ fl oz) sparkling water

Place the geranium sprigs in a jug with the orange
blossom water and top with the sparkling water.
Serve over ice.

MUDDLED BERRY FIZZ

Makes: *750 ml (25½ fl oz)*
Takes: *10 minutes*

200 g (7 oz) frozen mixed berries
1 teaspoon natural vanilla paste
1 tablespoon agave syrup
750 ml (25½ fl oz) sparkling water

Muddle the berries in the bottom of a jug.
Add the vanilla paste and agave, and top with
the sparkling water.

ORANGE AND TURMERIC FIZZ

Makes: *750 ml (25½ fl oz)*
Takes: *10 minutes*

juice of 1 orange
½–1 teaspoon ground turmeric, to taste
1 tablespoon Honey Syrup (optional) (p. 62)
1 orange, sliced into half-rounds
750 ml (25½ fl oz) sparkling water

Combine the orange juice and turmeric powder to taste in a jug and mix well. Add the honey syrup, if using, and the sliced oranges, then top with the sparkling water.

APPLE AND PEAR FIZZ

Makes: *750 ml (25½ fl oz)*
Takes: *10 minutes, plus overnight to infuse*

1 apple, cored and sliced
1 pear, cored and sliced
juice of ½ lemon
750 ml (25½ fl oz) sparkling water

Place the sliced apple and pear in a 1 litre (34 fl oz) glass jar or bottle and add the lemon juice and sparkling water. Refrigerate overnight. Serve simply, over ice.

WATERMELON FIZZ

Makes: *750 ml (25½ fl oz)*
Takes: *5 minutes*

200 g (7 oz) watermelon, sliced into wedges
2 mint sprigs
750 ml (25½ fl oz) sparkling water

Place the watermelon and mint sprigs in a jug and top with the sparkling water.

ABOUT THE AUTHOR

Kathy Kordalis is a London-based food-stylist and recipe writer. She has worked in the food industry for years and her experience includes managing the Divertimenti Cookery School and training as a chef at the Leiths School of Food and Wine. Her approach to food is light, relaxed and accessible, drawing inspiration from her classical training in London, along with her Australian and Mediterranean heritage. It's all about sharing with friends and family, and coming up with new recipes to excite them! This is Kathy's fifth book.

ACKNOWLEDGEMENTS

Thank you to the fabulous Kate Pollard, Kajal Mistry and the Hardie Grant team for giving me the opportunity to write this book.

The amazing Jacqui Melville whose creative vision, skill and technique really elevated all the images as well being such a blast to work with.

Thank you also to Prop stylist Pene Parker, Assistant Esther Clark and the wonderful Joana Ferreira!

INDEX

A

agave syrup
Cayenne Pepper and Agave
Tequila 120
Cranberry-spiced Whiskey 42
Muddled Berry Fizz 132
almonds: Homemade Amaretto 90
Alpine Rocks 70
amaretto: Homemade Amaretto 90
Angelica and Orris Root Gin 101
Angostura bitters
Cherry Chocolate Cocktail 82
Cherry Gin Sling 38
Jasmine Sour 48
Juniper Mule 73
Maple Walnut 89
Marvin 26
Oregano Pisco Sour 56
Peace 61
Aperol: Rose Aperol Spritz 47
apple cider vinegar
Apple and Fennel Shrub 131
Cranberry and Clove Shrub 131
Pomegranate Shrub 131
apple juice: Apple and Juniper Fizz 73
apples
Apple and Fennel Shrub 131
Apple and Pear Fizz 135
Apple Sparkle 34
Green Apple, Ginger and Yuzu
Vodka 34
apricots: Peach and Apricot
Armagnac 26
aquavit
Blood Orange Mary with Aquavit 55
Fennel and Cardamom Aquavit 55
Lingonberry Aquavit 55
Armagnac
Champeach 26
Marvin 26
Peach and Apricot Armagnac 26
aromatics 8

B

Basil Rum 65
bay leaves: Roasted Lemon and
Bay Vodka 61
beetroot
Beet Jax 97
Beetroot and Sour Cherry Vodka 97
Benedictine: Walnut Cognac 89
berries, mixed: Muddled Berry Fizz 132
blackberries
Blackberry and Thyme Syrup 127
Tangerine and Blackberry Fizz 132
Blood Orange Mary with Aquavit 55

blueberries: Violet and Blueberry
Vodka 50–1
botanicals 10
bourbon
Chai Bourbon Sour 112
Cherry Chocolate Cocktail 82
Chocolate Bourbon 82
Spiked Salted-Caramel Affogato 82
Star Anise and Maple Bourbon 112
brandy
Brandy Julep 25
Brandytopf 25
Espresso Martini 81
Hazelnut Liqueur 94
Tonka Bean Brandy 81
Walnut Cognac 89
Bumbo 86

C

cacao nibs: Chocolate Bourbon 82
Campari: The Jasmine 48
Canchànchara 77
cardamom pods
Chocolate Bourbon 82
Cranberry-spiced Whiskey 42
Fennel and Cardamom Aquavit 55
Cayenne Pepper and Agave Tequila 120
Chai Bourbon Sour 112
Chamomile Syrup 128
Champagne
Champeach 26
Orange Fizz 17
Violet Blueberry Champagne with
Sorbet 50–1
Champeach 26
Chartreuse: Morning After 90
cherries
Beetroot and Sour Cherry Vodka 97
Cherry Chocolate Cocktail 82
Cherry Gin 38
Cherry Gin Sling 38
Cherry Syrup 38
chillies 10
Jalapeño Vodka 116
Mexican Revolver 22
Red Chilli and Passion Fruit
Mezcal 119
Smoky Ancho Chilli and Grapefruit
Rum 115
Chocolate Bourbon 81
cider: Hazelnut Cider 94
cinnamon
Cinnamon and Nutmeg Dark
Rum 86
Cranberry-spiced Whiskey 42
Star Anise and Maple Bourbon 112
citrus fruit
Brandytopf 25

Marma-ade 17
Smoked Rosemary Rum 69
clementines: Marma-ade 17
cloves
Cranberry and Clove Shrub 131
Star Anise and Maple Bourbon 112
Cobbler 56
cocktails
Alpine Rocks 70
Apple and Juniper Fizz 73
The Apple Blossom 34
Apple Sparkle 34
Beet Jax 97
Black Peppercorn and Strawberry
Vodka 123
Blood Orange Mary with Aquavit 55
Brandy Julep 25
Bumbo 86
Canchànchara 77
Chai Bourbon Sour 112
Champeach 26
Cherry Chocolate Cocktail 82
Cherry Gin Sling 38
Cobbler 56
The Cranberry Spice 42
Cranberry-spiced Whiskey 42
Cucumber and Ginger Sparkle 33
Dirty Martini 102
Dirty Watermelon and Cucumber
Juice 102
Don Diabolo 119
Espresso Martini 81
Gin and Grapefruit Gimlet 62
Hazelnut Cider 94
Horseradish, Raspberry and Peach
Vodka 108
Hot Buttered Rum 86
Jalapeño Daisy 116
The Jasmine 48
Jasmine Sour 48
Juniper Mule 73
Lime and Lemongrass Rum Jug 18
Lingonberry Aquavit 55
Liquorice Stick Cocktail 78
Mango Hot Mama 120
Mangosit 52
Mango-tini 29
Maple Walnut 89
Marvin 26
Melon Cucumber-tini 30
Melon Patch 30
Mexican Revolver 22
Mint, Pomegranate and Fig Gin 66
Morning After 90
Orange Fizz 17
Oregano Pisco Sour 56
Peace 61
Peach and Mango Sangria 29

Pineapple Margarita 107
Pink Hibiscus 21
Pistachio Rose Mule 93
Pomrum 77
Queen Victoria's Tonic 101
Rose Aperol Spritz 47
Saffron Cooler 98
Smoked Rosemary Rum 69
Spicy Grapefruit and Chipotle
    Cocktail 115
Spiked Raspberry Soda 41
Spiked Salted-Caramel Affogato 82
Strawberry and Basil Daiquiri 65
Summertime Garden Shrub 37
Sweet and Sour Strawberry Rhubarb
    Daiquiri 36–7
Tropical Fruit Rum Jug 85
Verbena Cocktail 22
Violet Blueberry Champagne with
    Sorbet 50–1
Wasabi Spice 111
coconut water: Tropical Fruit Rum
    Jug 85
coffee: Morning After 90
Cognac
    Maple Walnut 89
    Walnut Cognac 89
Cointreau
    Cherry Gin Sling 38
    The Jasmine 48
coriander seeds
    Angelica and Orris Root Gin 101
    Cucumber, Lime and
        Coriander-seed Gin 33
Cranberry and Clove Shrub 131
Cranberry-spiced Whiskey 42
cucumber
    Cucumber and Ginger Sparkle 33
    Cucumber, Lime and
        Coriander-seed Gin 33
    Dirty Watermelon and Cucumber
        Juice 102
    Melon Cucumber-tini 30
    Turmeric and Pickled Dill
        Cucumber Vodka 102
    Wasabi, Ginger and Cucumber
        Gin 111
    Wasabi Spice 111

D
Dirty Martini 102
Dirty Watermelon and Cucumber
    Juice 102
Don Diabolo 119

E
elderflower cordial: Jasmine Tea and
    Elderflower Gin 48

elderflower liqueur: Queen Victoria's
    Tonic 101
Espresso Martini 81
F
fennel
    Apple and Fennel Shrub 131
    Fennel and Cardamom Aquavit 55
figs: Mint, Pomegranate and Fig Gin 66
flavourings 8, 10
fruits 10. see also citrus fruit;
    Tropical fruit

G
Geranium Fizz 132
gin
    Angelica and Orris Root Gin 101
    Apple and Juniper Fizz 73
    Cherry Gin 38
    Cherry Gin Sling 38
    Cucumber and Ginger Sparkle 33
    Cucumber, Lime and
        Coriander-seed Gin 33
    Gin and Grapefruit Gimlet 62
    The Jasmine 48
    Jasmine Sour 48
    Jasmine Tea and Elderflower Gin 48
    Juniper and Vanilla Gin 73
    Juniper Mule 73
    Lemon Thyme and Honey-infused
        Gin 62
    Mint, Pomegranate and Fig Gin 66
    Pink Grapefruit and Hibiscus Tea
        Gin 21
    Pink Hibiscus 21
    Pistachio Gin 93
    Pistachio Rose Mule 93
    Queen Victoria's Tonic 101
    Saffron Cooler 98
    Saffron Gin 98
    Wasabi, Ginger and Cucumber
        Gin 111
    Wasabi Spice 111
ginger
    Green Apple, Ginger and Yuzu
        Vodka 34
    Kaffir Lime, Lemongrass and Ginger
        Rum 52
    Wasabi, Ginger and Cucumber
        Gin 111
ginger beer
    Cucumber and Ginger Sparkle 33
    Don Diabolo 119
    Juniper Mule 73
    Pistachio Rose Mule 93
ginger syrup
    Verbena Cocktail 22
    Wasabi Spice 111
Grand Marnier: Spicy Grapefruit and

Chipotle Cocktail 115
grapefruit
    Gin and Grapefruit Gimlet 62
    Pink Grapefruit and Hibiscus Tea
        Gin 21
    Rose, Strawberry and Red
        Grapefruit Wine 47
    Smoky Ancho Chilli and Grapefruit
        Rum 115
    Tropical Rum 85
grapes: Petimezi Syrup 128
Green Melon Vodka 30

H
Hazelnut Cider 94
Hazelnut Liqueur 94
herbs 10
hibiscus tea: Pink Grapefruit And
    Hibiscus Tea Gin 21
honey
    honey syrup 62
    Lemon Thyme and Honey-infused
        Gin 62
Honeycomb-infused Dark Rum 77
Horseradish, Raspberry and Peach
    Vodka 108
Hot Buttered Rum 86

I
infusion 6, 12

J
Jalapeño Daisy 116
Jalapeño Vodka 116
The Jasmine 48
Jasmine Sour 48
Jasmine Tea and Elderflower Gin 48
juniper berries
    Angelica and Orris Root Gin 101
    Juniper and Vanilla Gin 73
    Juniper Mule 73

K
Kaffir Lime, Lemongrass and Ginger
    Rum 52

L
Lemon Thyme and Honey-infused
    Gin 62
Lemon Verbena Syrup 127
Lemon Verbena Tequila 22
lemongrass
    Kaffir Lime, Lemongrass and
        Ginger Rum 52
    Lime And Lemongrass Rum 18
lemons
    Mango-tini 29
    Oregano and Lemon-infused Pisco 56

Roasted Lemon and Bay Vodka 61

limes
    Cucumber, Lime and Coriander-seed
        Gin 33
    Green Melon Vodka 30
    Lime and Lemongrass Rum 18
    Lime aLemongrass Rum Jug 18
    Oregano Pisco Sour 56
    Tropical Rum 85
Lingonberry Aquavit 55
liqueurs 6
    Hazelnut Liqueur 94
Liquorice Stick Cocktail 78
Liquorice Whiskey 78
lychee syrup: Tropical Rum 85

M
Madeira: Peace 61
mangoes
    Mango and Tarragon Vodka 29
    Mango Hot Mama 120
    Mango-tini 29
    Mangosit 52
maple syrup
    Chocolate Bourbon 82
    Cinnamon and Nutmeg Dark Rum 86
    Star Anise and Maple Bourbon 112
Maple Walnut 89
Marma-ade 17
Marvin 26
melons
    Dirty Watermelon and Cucumber
        Juice 102
    Green Melon Vodka 30
    Melon Cucumber-tini 30
    Melon Patch 30
    Saffron Cooler 98
    Watermelon Fizz 135
Mexican Revolver 22
mezcal
    Don Diabolo 119
    Red Chilli and Passion Fruit
        Mezcal 119
Midori: Green Melon Vodka 30
mint
    Mint, Pomegranate and Fig Gin 66
    Watermelon Fizz 135
Morning After 90
Muddled Berry Fizz 132

N
nutmeg: Cinnamon and Nutmeg Dark
    Rum 86

O
orange blossom water

Geranium Fizz 132
Marma-ade 17
Orange Fizz 17
oranges
    Blood Orange Mary with Aquavit 55
    Marma-ade 17
    Orange and Turmeric Fizz 135
    Orange Fizz 17
    Violet and Blueberry Vodka 50–1
Oregano and Lemon-infused Pisco 56
Oregano Pisco Sour 56
orris root powder: Angelica and Orris
    Root Gin 101

P
passion fruit:
    Red Chilli and Passion Fruit
        Mezcal 119
Peace 61
peaches
    Horseradish, Raspberry and Peach
        Vodka 108
    Peach and Apricot Armagnac 26
    Peach and Mango Sangria 29
pears: Apple and Pear Fizz 135
peppercorns
    Black Peppercorn and Strawberry
        Vodka 123
    Pink Peppercorn and Pineapple
        Tequila 107
Petimezi Syrup 128
Pine Vodka 70
pineapple
    Pineapple Margarita 107
    Pink Peppercorn and Pineapple
        Tequila 107
Pink Hibiscus 21
pisco
    Cobbler 56
    Oregano and Lemon-infused Pisco 56
    Oregano Pisco Sour 56
Pistachio Gin 93
Pistachio Rose Mule 93
pomegranates
    Mint, Pomegranate and Fig Gin 66
    Pomegranate Shrub 131
    Pomrum 77
Pomrum 77
prosecco: Mexican Revolver 22

Q
Queen Victoria's Tonic 101

R
raspberries
    Horseradish, Raspberry and Peach
        Vodka 108
    Raspberry, Redcurrant and Vanilla

Vodka 41
    Spiked Raspberry Soda 41
redcurrants: Raspberry, Redcurrant and
    Vanilla Vodka 41
rhubarb: Strawberry and Rhubarb
    Rum 36–7
rose petals
    Pistachio Gin 93
    Rose Syrup 127
rosé wine
    Rose Aperol Spritz 47
    Rose, Strawberry and Red Grapefruit
        Wine 47
rosemary: Smoked Rosemary Rum 69
rosewater: Rose Syrup 127
rum
    Basil Rum 65
    Brandy Julep 25
    Bumbo 86
    Canchànchara 77
    Cinnamon and Nutmeg Dark Rum 86
    Honeycomb-infused Dark Rum 77
    Hot Buttered Rum 86
    Kaffir Lime, Lemongrass and Ginger
        Rum 52
    Lime And Lemongrass Rum 18
    Lime and Lemongrass Rum Jug 18
    Mango Hot Mama 120
    Mangosit 52
    Morning After 90
    Pomrum 77
    Smoked Rosemary Rum 69
    Smoky Ancho Chilli and Grapefruit
        Rum 115
    Spicy Grapefruit and Chipotle
        Cocktail 115
    Strawberry and Basil Daiquiri 65
    Strawberry and Rhubarb Rum 36–7
    Summertime Garden Shrub 37
    Sweet and Sour Strawberry Rhubarb
        Daiquiri 36–7
    Tropical Fruit Rum Jug 85
    Tropical Rum 85

S
Saffron Cooler 98
Saffron Gin 98
sangria: Peach and Mango Sangria 29
sherry: Saffron Cooler 98
shrubs 10
    Apple and Fennel Shrub 131
    Cranberry and Clove Shrub 131
    Pomegranate Shrub 131
    Strawberry and Rhubarb Shrub 36–7
Simple Syrup 127
Smoked Rosemary Rum 69
Smoky Ancho Chilli and Grapefruit
    Rum 115

soda water: Spiked Raspberry Soda 41
sparkling water 10
    Apple and Pear Fizz 135
    Apple Sparkle 34
    Geranium Fizz 132
    Muddled Berry Fizz 132
    Orange and Turmeric Fizz 135
    Tangerine and Blackberry Fizz 132
    Watermelon Fizz 135
spices 10
    Cranberry-spiced Whiskey 42
Spicy Grapefruit and Chipotle
    Cocktail 115
Spiked Raspberry Soda 41
Spiked Salted-Caramel Affogato 82
spirits 6, 8
star anise
    Cranberry-spiced Whiskey 42
    Star Anise and Maple Bourbon 112
strawberries
    Black Peppercorn and Strawberry
        Vodka 123
    Rose, Strawberry and Red Grapefruit
        Wine 47
    Strawberry and Basil Daiquiri 65
    Strawberry and Rhubarb Rum 36–7
sugar. see syrups
Sweet and Sour Strawberry Rhubarb
    Daiquiri 36–7
syrups 10
    Blackberry and Thyme Syrup 127
    Chamomile Syrup 128
    Cherry Syrup 38
    Honey Syrup 62
    Lemon Verbena Syrup 127
    Petimezi Syrup 128
    Pine Syrup 70
    Rose Syrup 127
    Simple Syrup 127
    Smoked Rosemary Citrus Syrup 69
    Violet Syrup 50–1
    Whiskey Syrup 128

T
Tangerine and Blackberry Fizz 132
tarragon: Mango and Tarragon Vodka 29
tea: Jasmine Tea and Elderflower Gin 48
tea syrup: Chai Bourbon Sour 112
tequila
    Cayenne Pepper and Agave
        Tequila 120
    Lemon Verbena Tequila 22
    Mango Hot Mama 120
    Mexican Revolver 22
    Pineapple Margarita 107
    Pink Peppercorn and Pineapple
        Tequila 107
    Verbena Cocktail 22

thyme: Blackberry and Thyme Syrup 127
Tia Maria: Espresso Martini 81
Tonka Bean Brandy 81
Tropical Fruit Rum Jug 85
Tropical Rum 85
turmeric
    Orange and Turmeric Fizz 135
    Turmeric and Pickled Dill Cucumber
        Vodka 102

V
vanilla pods
    Chocolate Bourbon 82
    Cranberry-spiced Whiskey 42
    Hazelnut Liqueur 94
    Juniper and Vanilla Gin 73
    Pistachio Gin 93
    Raspberry, Redcurrant and Vanilla
        Vodka 41
    Roasted Lemon and Bay Vodka 61
vegetables 10
Verbena Cocktail 22
vermouth
    Beet Jax 97
    Cobbler 56
    Dirty Martini 102
    Marma-ade 17
    Pink Hibiscus 21
viognier: Peach and Mango Sangria 29
Violet and Blueberry Vodka 50–1
Violet Blueberry Champagne with
    Sorbet 50–1
vodka
    Alpine Rocks 70
    The Apple Blossom 34
    Apple Sparkle 34
    Beet Jax 97
    Beetroot and Sour Cherry Vodka 97
    Black Peppercorn and Strawberry
        Vodka 123
    Dirty Martini 102
    Dirty Watermelon and Cucumber
        Juice 102
    Green Apple, Ginger and Yuzu
        Vodka 34
    Green Melon Vodka 30
    Hazelnut Cider 94
    Hazelnut Liqueur 94
    Homemade Amaretto 90
    Horseradish, Raspberry and Peach
        Vodka 108
    Jalapeño Daisy 116
    Jalapeño Vodka 116
    Mango and Tarragon Vodka 29
    Mango-tini 29
    Marma-ade 17
    Melon Cucumber-tini 30
    Melon Patch 30

Morning After 90
Orange Fizz 17
Peace 61
Peach and Mango Sangria 29
Pine Vodka 70
Raspberry, Redcurrant and
    Vanilla Vodka 41
Roasted Lemon and Bay Vodka 61
Spiked Raspberry Soda 41
Turmeric and Pickled Dill Cucumber
    Vodka 102
Violet and Blueberry Vodka 50–1

W
Walnut Cognac 89
Wasabi, Ginger and Cucumber Gin 111
Wasabi Spice 111
water. see sparkling water
Watermelon Fizz 135
whiskey
    The Cranberry Spice
    Cranberry-spiced Whiskey 42
    Liquorice Stick Cocktail 78
    Liquorice Whiskey 78
    Whiskey Syrup 128
wine
    Cranberry-spiced Whiskey 42
    Rose Aperol Spritz 47
    Rose, Strawberry and Red Grapefruit
        Wine 47

Y
yuzu juice
    Green Apple, Ginger and Yuzu
        Vodka 34
    Jalapeño Daisy 116
    Verbena Cocktail 22

INFUSED
BOOZE

◇◇◇

Kathy Kordalis

First published in 2018 by Hardie Grant Books,
an imprint of Hardie Grant Publishing

Hardie Grant Books (UK)
52–54 Southwark Street
London SE1 1UN

Hardie Grant Books (Australia)
Ground Floor, Building 1
658 Church Street
Melbourne, VIC 3121

hardiegrantbooks.com

The moral rights of Kathy Kordalis to be identified
as the author of this work has been asserted by her
in accordance with the Copyright, Designs and
Patents Act 1988.

Text © Kathy Kordalis

British Library Cataloguing-in-Publication Data.
A catalogue record for this book is available from
the British Library.

ISBN: 978-1-78488-152-8

Publisher: Kate Pollard
Senior Editor: Kajal Mistry
Desk Editor: Molly Ahuja
Publishing Assistant: Eila Purvis
Cover and Internal Design: Stuart Hardie
Photography © Jacqui Melville
Prop stylist: Pene Parker and Ginger Whisk
Copy editor: Andrea O'Connor
Proofreader: Emily Preece-Morrison
Indexer: Cathy Heath
Colour Reproduction by p2d
Printed and bound in China by 1010